# Championship
# SNOOKER

# Championship
# SNOOKER

## TERRY GRIFFITHS
### with Clive Everton

Queen Anne Press
Macdonald Futura Publishers
London

# Acknowledgements

The publishers gratefully acknowledge the following for photographs used in this book: Western Mail & Echo Limited, pages 10, 39;. Eamon McCabe/Professional Sport, pages 42, 60, 102, 108, 129, 136; Irwyn Morgan, page 47; The Citizen, Johannesburg, page 52; Neil Wigley, page 61; White's Newsagency, page 70; Dave Muscroft, cover photographs and pages 112 and 134.

Line drawings by Bert Hackett
Table diagrams by Jack Fitzmaurice

First published in 1981 by Queen Anne Press, Macdonald Futura Publishers Limited, Paulton House, 8 Shepherdess Walk, London N1 7LW

ISBN 0362 00543 5

Filmset by SIOS Limited

Printed and bound in Great Britain by Richard Clay (The Chaucer Press) Limited, Bungay, Suffolk

# Contents

# —————1—————
# Introduction

The public loves a fairytale and Terry Griffiths gave them one. In April 1979, less than eight months after packing up his job as an insurance agent, he won the World Professional Snooker Championship at his first attempt in front of a full house at the Crucible Theatre, Sheffield, and 9.8 million television viewers. It was, said Fred Davis, from his vantage point of fifty years as a professional, 'the greatest achievement the game has ever known'.

Like all good fairytales this one has a moral: anybody can change his life if he has the talent, the will and the nerve. For the snooker world it had the further merit of hammering another nail into the cliché with which generations of headmasters have put down kids fascinated by the multi-coloured equations of the green baize game: 'Proficiency at billiards is a sign of a misspent youth.' When Griffiths – clean cut, unassuming and brave – won the world title it was impossible for any headmaster to decry such a hero or the game he played.

When Griffiths started playing, amateur snooker was very localised. There were few opportunities to make a wide reputation and the professional ranks were so tightly knit that a career in the game was hardly feasible. A few cups or making a few bob playing for money in the local billiard hall was as much as one's cue could be expected to earn. As world champion, his income immediately soared to more than £50,000 a year.

When he reached the final of the Welsh Amateur Championship in 1972, at his first attempt, the first tremors of the snooker boom were being felt. The game was beginning to benefit from government aid and commercial sponsorship, so that amateur governing bodies like the Welsh Billiards and Snooker Association, hitherto struggling, suddenly had the means with which to develop it.

Both the amateur and professional circuits have expanded so much that snooker now offers the big money potential of sports like golf and tennis. It has started to supersede boxing as the classic way of fighting your way out of an underprivileged or limiting environment though, ironically, the last thing Griffiths wants is to leave his beloved Llanelli. 'I was born here. I'll probably die here. I know everybody round here.

Everybody knows me.' The only thing he doesn't like about Llanelli is that it seems to be a long way from anywhere else. In the twelve weeks following his 1979 championship win (including two when he had chicken pox and didn't budge from his house), he travelled seventeen thousand miles.

The strains of championship snooker and of a champion's life are greater than they have ever been. In the age of Joe Davis, the world championship was a season-long event. Each match took 73 frames, spread over a week, to decide. The final lasted two weeks and 145 frames. The very length of the matches made close finishes rare, the pressure less intense. There were, in any case, fewer players of the highest quality. The game's financial structure would not have supported them, which is perhaps why they did not emerge.

Nowadays, the world championship is crammed into a fortnight – the champion has to win at least four matches in this period – and the calendar is full of important supporting events. What time is left tends to go on exhibition engagements in clubs, so well paid that only those with the strongest wills can resist cramming their diaries with them.

The pressure, not just of the matches but of the life the professional must lead, has escalated with the rewards. Success depends on how well a player copes with the internal and external pressures he faces. He cannot begin to do this unless his technique is fundamentally sound.

*Championship Snooker* is not the sort of book which implies that you can be a novice at page one and a champion by the time you've completed it – but the section in which Griffiths analyses his technique is designed to have a strong instructional content for those who have a mind to absorb it. There is never anything to be lost by going back to basics, for good amateur players often lose their way through neglecting to follow precepts of which they have known the truth since their earliest experience of the game. Sometimes, too, a champion's dissection of his own technique can reveal new pathways to improvement.

Championships are not, of course, won through technique alone. The physical equivalent of chess, snooker similarly demands a high degree of sophistication in shot selection, considering whether to endanger the certainty of potting a ball in an attempt to gain positional advantage, choosing the moment to chance your arm or await a better opportunity, balancing possible risk against possible gain, seeking ways to exert pressure rather than having to respond to it.

Table diagrams are nothing new in snooker books, but *Championship Snooker* does attempt some more detailed sequences than have ever appeared before, in order to discuss some of the less obvious factors which determine whether vital championship frames are won or lost. Here again, as with other sequences which illustrate the compilation of notable breaks, the lessons are there if you care to find them.

# INTRODUCTION

Much was made of Griffiths's overnight rise to fame but in reality no one plays in, let alone wins, a world championship without crystallising to best advantage a mass of accumulated experience. In recalling what now seem obscure early struggles, it is possible to trace the elements of a snooker player's education, a process which the thinking player continues until he puts his cue in his case for the last time.

Whatever he achieves, though, the snooker world will always see Griffiths at the Crucible Theatre, Sheffield, at twenty-to-two in the morning after he had beaten the Australian, Eddie Charlton, 19-17 in their 1979 world semi-final. Light-headed with the inexpressible relief of tension after three days battling – nine hours that day – deafened by the ovation from everyone who had stayed, hoping that the newcomer from nowhere could do it while believing in their hearts that it was too much to ask, he walked up and down in his short-stepped, springy way, swinging his arms as if lost for a means of conveying his joy. His account of the match poured into David Vine's microphone until, in one identifiable second, with pride and wonderment mixed, the reality hit him: 'I'm in the final, now, you know', he said.

For all the champagne and jubilation of his victory over Dennis Taylor, the final was in many respects an anti-climax. The Griffiths v Charlton semi-final was, for most of the snooker fraternity, the final, because it was sensed that this match would decide what sort of champion the game would have: Charlton, dour, solid, consistent, the archetypal tough pro, an establishment figure through and through; or Griffiths, still enough in touch with the innocent feelings with which all players start the long competitive road to be high on the adventure of it all, willing to chance an arm unencumbered by the weight of previous failures or near misses.

On the table, Griffiths was perfectly self-possessed. Sitting out, he studied, when he sensed it was important, the game or his opponent; otherwise he sang soundlessly in his mind (often his favourite song, *Myfanwy*), or simply excluded everything from his cocoon of concentration, achieving a harmony of his mind, in his inner game, which is the sportsman's optimum state. 'I was able to shut off completely from anything I didn't want. I've never done that, never, ever before.'

CLIVE EVERTON

# 2

# Control the Cue Ball, Control the Game

As so many players do, I began on a small table at home with my father. When I was fourteen, I started going into the local billiard hall in Llanelli with my mates, where I showed my cagey side by refusing to play anyone unless they gave me start. The tradition was that the loser paid for the table.

I picked up the game by trial and error, whereas the young players of today can see plenty of top-class snooker on television. They can see the professionals play to certain basic patterns and certain basic principles. Once they observe what is being done, they gain an idea of what to strive for. They may not have a clue about how to do it, but at least they will know what they need to find out.

Such increased opportunities to learn from top-class players help to explain why there are many more young players of century break standard than there used to be. Another reason is that the snooker boom has meant more snooker centres, more facilities and more chances to absorb knowledge at first hand from first class amateurs.

No one needs to watch snooker very long to realise that by far the most important of snooker's 22 balls is the white cue-ball. The player who best controls the cue-ball wins the game. He needs to strike it accurately enough to pot balls; and he needs to strike it at various speeds and with various spins to control its position in such a way as to give himself a sequence of relatively easy shots, rather than one difficult shot after another.

Unless a player can strike the white accurately, he will not consistently be able to make it contact the object-ball at the angle necessary to pot it. His eyesight may assess the potting angle correctly; but if he thinks he is striking the cue-ball plumb centre, when in fact he is striking it a little to the left or right, he is imparting spin unintentionally. Unless cue-ball and object-ball are very close together or unless the object ball is hanging over a pocket, this unintentional spin will cause the cue-ball to drift from its intended path. The pot will be missed, for by the time the cue-ball reaches the object-ball, the contact will occur at the wrong angle.

Thus a snooker player cannot reach the top without a reliable cue action, which will enable him to concentrate on the problems of the game itself secure in the knowledge that he is mechanically delivering the cue through straight and true. But no player is a machine. Therefore, his aim must be to reduce the margin of human error by planning to make each successive shot relatively easy. It is in this 'second phase' of cue-ball control that the art of the game is exhibited at its highest level.

Such control is achieved through the two basic skills – strength of shot and spin. Most players develop enough 'touch' or 'feel' to use more or less the right amount of power to send the cue-ball varying distances. However, it is the study of a lifetime for the mind constantly to work out other variables like the degree to which contact between cue-ball and object-ball affects the cue-ball's momentum or angle.

Diagram 1 shows a side view of the three points at which the tip of the cue may strike the cue-ball.

Point A is dead centre: no top spin; no back spin; no side spin. This is known as a plain ball shot.

Point B is where the tip strikes the cue-ball to produce maximum top spin. When the cue-ball strikes the object-ball on a straight pot the 'top' will then exaggerate the natural tendency to follow behind it.

Point C is very important. It is the point at which the tip strikes the cue-ball to produce maximum back-spin, known in snooker circles as 'screw'.

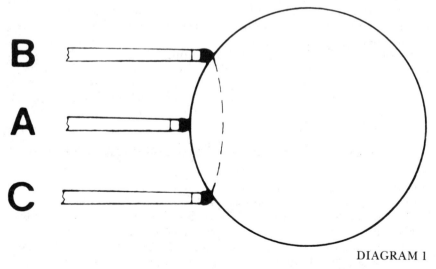

DIAGRAM 1

If you use screw on a straight pot, the cue-ball will come back on the same straight line after striking the object-ball. How far you can make it come back will depend partly on the power behind the shot but more on true cueing – in other words, really striking where you think you are striking, and making the cue follow through smoothly so that the rounded, dome-shaped surface of the tip makes a smooth, almost caressing contact with the rounded surface of the ball.

When the pot is not dead straight, the player can only 'screw' back at an angle. As the cue-ball is not striking the full weight of the object-ball but only a segment of it, it becomes more difficult to get the screw to take effect because there is less ball to bite on. The thinner the potting angle, the less it is possible to screw. That is why you will see professionals, when they are attempting to compile a break with a sequence of reds and blacks, playing so that they leave the cue-ball at the sort of angle on the black shown in diagram 2. Depending on precisely where the reds are situated, the player, in potting the black, can manipulate the cue-ball at any angle between point A and point E.

The cue-ball would reach point A if struck plain ball; it would need to be struck a fraction below centre and slightly more sharply to reach point B; lower still to reach point C. With even lower striking and a sharper 'nip' in the way the tip strikes the cue-ball, points D and E can be reached.

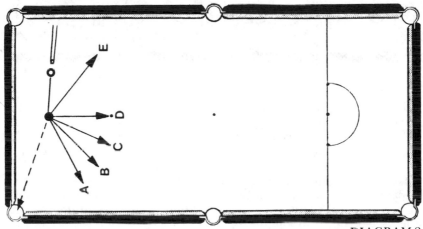

DIAGRAM 2

Diagram 3 (see next page) introduces the professional's other great aid to positional control – sidespin, or 'side'.

When the tip strikes the cue-ball wide of centre, it imparts spin – the wider of centre, the greater the spin. As I said earlier, unintentional side can cause you to miss pots and, even when you know you are using side, it usually makes pots more difficult. The professional, though, is constantly balancing in his mind just how much more difficult for himself he can afford to make the pot than it would be if he were not intent upon also setting up his cue-ball in prime position to continue his break.

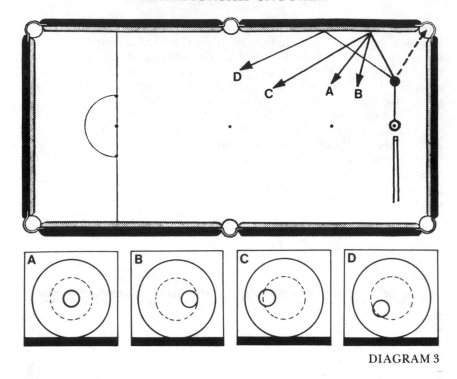

DIAGRAM 3

The diagram shows an easy pot with four different paths for the cue-ball to follow afterwards. The player, of course, chooses the one which best suits the development of his break.

Path A is for the plain shot ball. The cue-ball is struck at A. Path B shows how this angle is narrowed by the use of right-hand side, which makes the cue-ball check as it hits the cushion. The cue-ball is struck at B. Path C shows how the angle is widened by the use of left-hand side (see C) while path D shows how a combination of screw and left-hand side widens the angle still more.

One of the most difficult screw shots with side is shown in diagram 4. The player has an almost straight pot on the black, but a straight screw back will not enable the cue-ball to bounce off the cushion at the angle required to obtain position on the yellow. By playing the screw back with both screw and left-hand side, the cue-ball will spin off the cushion at a wider angle, as shown, to leave perfect position. This last shot is a test of cuemanship for anyone.

How does anyone get to that standard? Not necessarily through hard work. Many quite good players go adrift by losing sight of the fact that snooker is a game. Instead of just playing, they break it down into isolated parts, getting self-conscious and theoretical in the process.

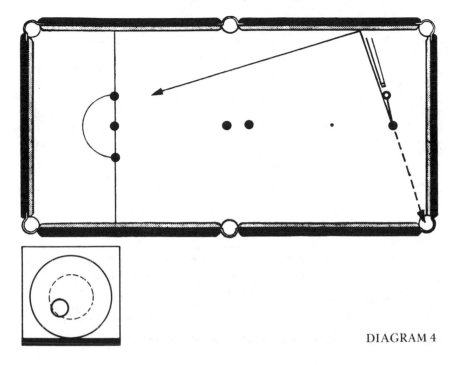

DIAGRAM 4

There are some books which recommend players to place the cue-ball on the brown spot and shoot it up the table over the blue, pink and black spots and back again. In this way, you can check whether you are striking the cue-ball plumb in the middle or whether you are a fraction out and thus imparting a touch of side unintentionally. As an occasional check, particularly for novices, this is all right; but if you do it a lot, you end up by wearing a faint line over the spots to remind you how well you can perform the exercise but no guarantee that you won't revert to off-centre striking when another ball is involved.

I am also very doubtful about the value of practising one shot dozens of times in succession. You might get it twenty consecutive times in practice, but how does this affect you if a similar shot comes up in a match? If it is one you were missing almost every time before your practice, you might approach it with more confidence, but you might also think: 'I've got this twenty times in practice. Wouldn't it be terrible to miss it now?' I've always avoided setting up the same shot time after time for that reason – I find it puts more pressure on if that particular shot comes up in a match.

Solo practice does have its place, and I do more on my own now than ever I did as an amateur. In fact it was quite late in my amateur career

15

before I practised on my own at all. Some of this practice is to find out exactly what happens in certain situations. Splitting a bunch of reds, for instance, is not just hitting and hoping but working out what is likely to happen if you take the cue-ball into the bunch in one way rather than another.

Certain departments of my game, like power run-throughs or middle pocket pots, are less strong than others but rather than play the same shot over and over I will play a lot of shots of the same type. Solo practice needs to be constructive, but if you make it drudgery it certainly won't be.

For a similar reason I believe it is very bad for young players to be brought up on tight tables, as they can develop bad habits which can last a lifetime. For example, players tend to make ultra-sure of their pots at the expense of the positional play which builds breaks. The idea that if you learn to cope with tight pockets then you will find the game simple with easier pockets doesn't work out, because you will have become so accustomed to devoting most of your attention to making sure of the pot that your range of positional shots tends to be very limited.

A player who is conditioned to regarding 25 as a substantial break will not readily adjust to the necessity of making 40s and 50s against an opponent who is used to making them. At championship level, players are always looking for the chance to compile breaks. Except in a once-in-a-thousand case, a break of 70 or more wins the game. If the balls are not positioned favourably enough for one frame-winning break, a 30-odd at the start and a 40-odd at the end should be enough to outweigh anything that happens in mid-frame.

In championship snooker, if you get an opening, you must make it count. There might not be another!

# 3

# My Technique and Yours

## THE GRIP

It has been said many times that you should grip the cue as if you are going to hit someone over the head with it. I can't put it any better than that, except to say that your grip should not be as tight or as fierce as it would be if you really were going to do that.

As drawing 1 shows, the grip is firm – in fact it should be just firm enough to pick the cue up from the table bed – but not so tight that it makes the wrist and hand muscles tense.

If you grip the cue too tightly, the tension in your hand will be transmitted all the way up your cue arm; and if your arm muscles are tense, your arm will move stiffly and jerkily rather than with the easy smoothness which gives the best results.

DRAWING 1

Equally, it is a mistake to grip too loosely. Some of the old billiards artists used very loose grips for their endless runs of close cannons, but these would be completely unsuited to snooker. Almost every shot at snooker is played firmly – even slow ones – so any looseness in the grip which allows the cue to give way even slightly on impact with the cue-ball is to be avoided.

I usually grip the cue with just an inch or so of the butt sticking out of the back of my cue hand. For some shots, for instance when I am stretching so much that I can only just reach the cue-ball comfortably, I might hold the cue at the very end. I might shorten my grip in certain other shots, perhaps if there were some obstructing balls or if I wanted to play a very delicate slow shot which travelled only a few inches, like rolling the cue-ball up for a snooker behind one of the small colours.

## THE BRIDGE

The most important factor in the bridge is that it should be steady. If it moves, even a fraction, it will affect the accuracy with which you strike the cue-ball and thus will in all probability cause you not to make the cue-ball/object-ball contact you intend.

Everyone at times finds difficulty in keeping his bridge perfectly steady – when bridging over a ball, for instance, or when hampered by a cushion – but in situations in which it is possible to place the whole hand firmly on the table, there is no reason why your bridge should not be rock solid.

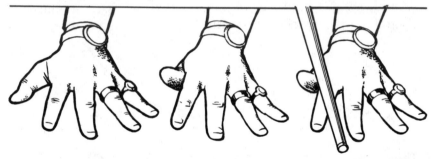

DRAWING 2

Place your bridge hand on the table (drawing 2) with the fingers widely spread, each gripping the cloth with the same strength. Cock the thumb and there is your bridge. Nothing could be much simpler, yet, until 1977, I didn't do this – and handicapped myself accordingly! I played with my fingers closed (drawing 3), thus making my bridge more fragile than it is now that it is more broadly based. As the drawing shows, the end of my thumb bends backwards naturally so this helps me to create a secure channel for my cue between thumb and fore-finger.

I was always able to run my cue straight and smooth through that channel but I came to realise that my bridge had certain limitations. I have smaller than average fingers – which can be useful in situations where the balls are spread in such a way that there is not much room to form my bridge where I want to – but I was making them into more of a disadvantage than they need have been.

By using the bridge with the fingers placed straight and flat I found that I had great limitations with run-through shots. My natural bridge was so low that I naturally struck the cue-ball below centre. I could also strike centre-ball when I wanted to, but there was just not enough height in my bridge to strike the cue-ball above centre to impart the top spin necessary for run-through shots.

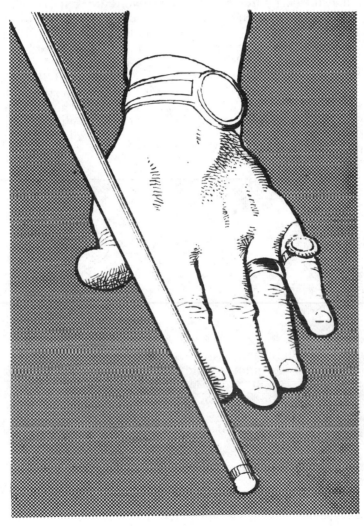

DRAWING 3

If I had been brought up on billiards where, for more shots than not, the cue-ball is struck centre-ball or above, I would not have got very far with my original bridge. But snooker is to a great extent a screw and stun game, so I was able to get away with it. I may say that a few players with big hands and thick fingers have the opposite problem: they naturally strike centre-ball and at times feel slightly awkward striking very low. Some of these players tilt their bridges on to the thumb for certain screw shots.

When I did decide to change my bridge, I worked very hard at developing my run-through shots. One shot I have practised for hours is to place cue-ball and object-ball about two feet apart, in a straight line to a top pocket about eight or nine feet away, and play not only the pot but to follow the cue-ball through into the pocket as well.

As drawing 4 shows, now my cue not only runs through the channel between thumb and forefinger but is given extra support by running across the forefinger. The wide-spread fingers should always grip the cloth firmly. The more power you are using for a shot the firmer this grip should be, so that the bridge does not move even fractionally as you thrust the cue forward.

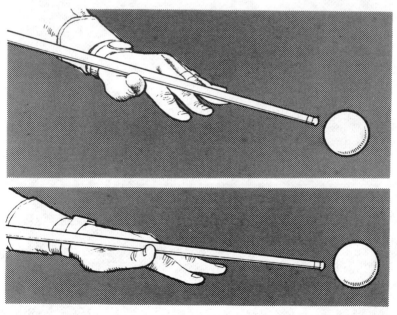

DRAWING 4

## STANCE

If you assess the angle for a pot correctly and bring your cue through straight, you will pot the ball virtually every time. When the margin for error is very small, as with many long-distance pots, the slightest miscalculation or the slightest deviation in true cueing will cause you to miss the shot.

A far more common cause of missing shots, though, is body or head movement on the shot, hence the importance of an absolutely solid stance. The body needs to be perfectly balanced so that it is possible to keep still even when playing the most forcing of shots. To achieve this, my feet are pointing in different directions (drawing 5), my left foot along the direction of the shot, my right leg sideways as a stabiliser. My weight is slightly forward: it needs to be, because it would inevitably come forward on a forcing shot anyway.

My front leg is, of course, slightly bent. The height of the cushions makes it impossible to get the cue truly horizontal to the line of the shot; but, by bending my front leg, I can comfortably get the cue as horizontal as is possible.

My rear leg is braced and straight. If I bring it forward of vertical, my stance becomes cramped and unsteady. If I take it backward of vertical,

DRAWING 5

21

I lose compactness. If the leg was back, inevitably some of my weight would be back, and when I wanted to play a forcing shot I would to some degree have to do so against the weight spread of my body.

From elbow to wrist, my cue arm is vertical too. If my cue hand were to start backward of vertical, my stroke would consist of virtually no backswing and almost all follow-through. If my cue hand started forward of vertical, the reverse would be true.

Standing sideways as I do involves a slight twist in my back. When you come to think of it, a great many sports actions – golf swings, tennis strokes, bowling in cricket – are performed with the body side on, and thus a twist in the back. In the great majority of cases, including my own, this sideways twist is natural and unthinking but I know of some players who to counteract pain or discomfort in their backs have gradually (and usually unconsciously) come round to a more 'front on' stance. In trying to protect their backs they have lost the true alignment of their cueing.

It is better to bend from the hips rather than the waist, as this throws less strain on the back. It is not a good idea to be carrying too much of a stomach as the weight of this, hanging forward, also puts the back under strain. I have had a few problems with back strain – in fact, three days before I played the 1977 English Amateur Championship final, I

DRAWING 6

couldn't get out of bed – and it's partly with this in mind that I watch my weight. I was once fifteen and a half stone but I now weigh twelve stone.

As drawing 6, showing my cue action at an angle from behind, illustrates, my cue is brushing lightly against my body. This helps prevent the cue wandering off line as it moves back and forth.

The head-on view (drawing 7) shows me looking down the cue through the middle of the cue-ball towards the point at which I want the cue-ball to contact the object-ball. I sight equally with both eyes so my chin is on my cue halfway between them.

DRAWING 7

You see most professionals and top amateurs sight in this way but it does not suit everybody's eyesight. Jonathan Barron, who won three English amateur titles, sighted under his right eye; Rex Williams sights under his left (as Joe Davis used to); and Graham Miles has his cue so far left of centre that it is almost under his ear. Eyesight sometimes changes. My fellow Welshman, Cliff Wilson, began his career with his cue between his eyes. In time, his left eye became considerably weaker so his cue is now directly under his right eye.

Ideally – say the purists – one should be able to draw a straight line from the point of aim, up the cue, through the sighting point (in my case between my eyes), through the shoulder to the point of the elbow of the cue arm. If all these are perfectly in line it is said that a player has a perfect 'line-up'.

John Spencer has one but Ray Reardon, who broke his shoulder when he was a boy, does not. Ray's elbow and wrist jut out but this does not seem to have prevented him from bringing his cue through straight. Fred Davis tends to have his elbow slightly tucked in so his wrist is turned slightly away from his body.

I have never considered this important. It can be reassuring to have a perfect line-up because mechanically this is obviously the soundest way to be – but players are not machines. As long as you can consistently deliver your cue through straight for all types of shot it doesn't matter how you do it. As with any sport, your natural co-ordination counts a lot more than contorting yourself into some pattern of orthodoxy which has been laid down by the theorists. As you can see, my own right shoulder is not directly behind my cue.

It is sensible to learn from example in terms of general principles, but as soon as you start moulding yourself into someone else's style you are likely to end up casting away what natural ability you have in favour of a style which may look correct but which, because it is not naturally your own, will break down under pressure. For example, some text-books recommend playing with the left arm thrust out straight, but this feels unnatural and uncomfortable to me. It is more likely to suit short players or tall players with short arms. I do like to have as much as possible of my lower arm resting on the table to give maximum steadiness.

## STRETCHING

There are some shots which you cannot reach with your normal stance. Some of these require the use of the rest – I will come to this special skill later – but many can be reached by stretching or by resting your body on the table.

Whatever body position you are forced to adopt, you must maintain your usual alignment of cue, sighting point and cue arm. Drawing 8 shows me at maximum stretch to my right. If the cue-ball was any

DRAWING 8

further to the right I would not be able to stretch far enough to get my cue arm behind the line of the shot, in which case I would use the rest.

Here, my upper body is turned to the right with my head and shoulders twisted to the left to allow me to look along the line of the shot. I have brought my right knee up on the table to improve my balance. If I bring my knee over, my hips and lower back automatically move in the same direction so my body is much steadier and better aligned than it would be if I kept both feet on the floor and simply stretched my body outwards.

Sometimes, of course, you will be forced into the latter alternative (drawing 9). The position of the other balls may be such that they are just where you want to put your knee! In this case, you have to do the best you can although there is a tendency to feel that your cue is hanging away from your body unsupported. If I could not get my knee on the table in this position I would probably use the rest.

DRAWING 9

DRAWING 10

Drawing 10 again shows me at full stretch, this time though with the table supporting all my body-weight. The rules of the game demand that contact is maintained with the floor, but in this case only the tip of my shoe is touching it. Sometimes a snag of lying on the table in this way, with your body so low (it has to rest on something at this angle), is that it can be awkward to lift the butt of the cue as high as is sometimes required.

In the position shown in drawing 11 (see next page) you see many players standing on their left leg with their right leg wavering in the air behind them. Occasionally, you are forced into this kind of stance, but the body position is inherently not as steady as it would be if the leg was resting on the table.

In the position I have adopted, with my left leg on the table, the additional support enables me to turn my upper body more easily. In this way, from my waist upwards, every aspect of my cueing is the same as it would be for an ordinary shot. It is only the position of the lower half of my body which has changed.

DRAWING 11

Occasionally, as drawing 12 shows, I will sit on the table to play my shot. This could be because there are balls other than cue-ball and object-ball preventing me from lying on the table, but there are also times when the cue-ball/object-ball angle is more accurately judged from an elevated position.

When cue-ball and object-ball are very close together, the potting angle can very easily be misjudged. The usual tendency is to make a thicker contact than one should. Fred Davis almost always plays with his chin well above his cue in such situations and so do I.

There is an additional complication, as shown in these drawings, because the cushion is preventing me placing my bridge hand for an orthodox bridge. I therefore have to place my hand on the cushion – which is higher than the table bed to start with – and strike downwards either through a thumb/first finger bridge (see left) or a loop bridge, which I tend to avoid (see right). You will notice how my cue is still kept on line through lightly brushing my waistcoat. Accurate centre-ball striking is vital in this sort of situation, for in striking downwards the smallest fraction of off-centre striking is magnified into an unintentional swerve shot.

The cushions and the middle pockets pose all sorts of bridging problems, many of which I seem to cope with better than most players because of my relatively short fingers. In only one of the positions

DRAWING 12

shown in drawing 13c (see next page), where I have to bridge awk-
wardly across a middle pocket, do I use a loop bridge which is resting
on my knuckles, almost a clenched fist bridge.

You will more often see players make loop bridges by tucking their
cue underneath the forefinger but I find that my method gives me a
more comfortable and thus more reliable hand position. Every player
should experiment with various ways to cope with these awkward
bridging positions. Players' hands are different shapes and sizes; some
are more supple than others. Never play a shot before your bridge
hand feels stable and steady.

On the first day of the 1980 World Professional Championship, Kirk
Stevens had made 136 and needed only the black for a new championship record break of 143 and a special £5,000 prize. The black was on
its spot but the cue-ball was almost in the jaws of a corner pocket. He
tried two or three different bridge hand positions without any of them

29

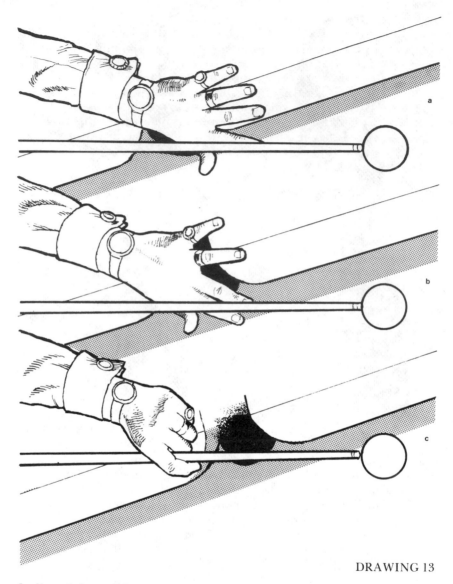

DRAWING 13

feeling right and then, over-anxious to get the black in, played the shot too hastily before he had settled his hand comfortably.

This brings up another great danger with awkward bridges: the player is so conscious that his bridge is not as comfortable as he would like it to be that he either rushes the shot or, in his anxiety to see the result of it, allows his head or body to move.

In drawings 13a and 13b I am again impeded by a middle pocket but in both cases I manage to make something resembling my normal bridge. In 13b the weight of my bridge rests on my first two fingers, the only two there is room for on the table bed. The heel of my hand is resting on the pocket. In 13a I cannot get any of my fingers on the table. The curve of the cushion as it turns into the middle pocket makes it very difficult to rest the cue on the cushion and make a loop bridge on top of it, so I simply use what is as near as possible my normal basic bridge. Inevitably, I have to raise my bridge and strike downwards: this is not ideal but, for me, it is better than any alternative.

Table designs vary and there are several ways in which the middle pockets can be set. Some have brass fittings on top which accentuate the degree to which you have to point your cue downwards. Others have the pocket backs set so far back that you can feel at times that your cue is bridging across a small chasm. Occasionally, the pocket leathers may be imperfectly fitted. Gary Owen, who lives in Australia now but was born in Llanelli and won two world amateur titles when he was a fireman in Birmingham, is fond of telling the tale of his second 147 maximum. The final black was on its spot but the cue-ball was only a few inches out from the middle pocket. As he tried to run his cue obliquely across the middle pocket he found that the leather was in such a state, sticky and misshapen, that he couldn't. He had a couple of tries, hesitated and then had a brainwave. He placed his handkerchief across the pocket, found that his cue would now run smoothly, and cut the black in clean as a whistle.

As in any other sport, sometimes you have to improvise. In terms of awkward bridges and stretches, this happens far more often at snooker than it ever did at billiards simply because there are more balls on the table. A player might use his natural bridge ninety per cent of the time in a game of billiards but at snooker, with so many balls about, his bridge is much more frequently hampered and he more often has to worry about fouling a ball as he leans over. A snooker player has to be very flexible and adaptable to cope with all these distractions.

On top of all this, a snooker player will often find himself playing with the cue-ball tight under the cushion either because he has left it there himself with a poor positional shot or, more likely, because his opponent has put it there with a safety shot. However true a player's cue action, there is always a chance of forcing him into a mistake if he is left with the cue-ball under the cushion and the object-ball several feet away.

If the cue-ball is in this position, only the top segment of the ball is hittable. Your range of shots is very restricted. It is impossible to get the cue truly horizontal but I get mine as horizontal as I can (see drawing

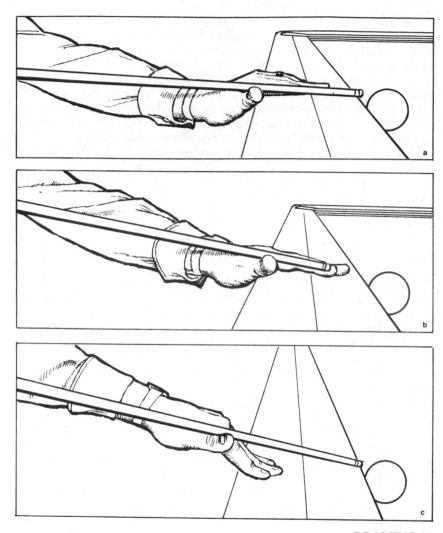

DRAWING 14

14a). Some professionals raise the butt of the cue more than I do, digging down into the ball (14b). This may reduce the chance of the type of miscue which occurs if the tip strikes the cushion before the ball, but it means that you are looking down at the cue-ball rather than along the line of the shot. By striking down at the cue-ball you also press it into the bed of the table so that it bounces slightly on its way to the object-ball. This does not assist accuracy.

# MY TECHNIQUE AND YOURS

In order to make my bridge as stable as possible, I like to get all four fingers flat on the cushion rail. My cue does not run across my first finger, as it does in a normal bridge, but is kept on line by running against my first finger. The thumb keeps it on line from the other side. My weight is forward so that I am almost pushing against the cushion rail. As my bridge is nearer the cue-ball than it would normally be, I shorten the grip on my cue. A good foot of the cue sticks out behind my cue-hand (drawing 15).

In drawing 14c the butt of my cue is raised because I am playing a shot which requires more power. If I need even more power, I will bring my bridge back to the edge of the cushion rail and rest it as steadily as I can on just my finger tips. It is, of course, impossible to use

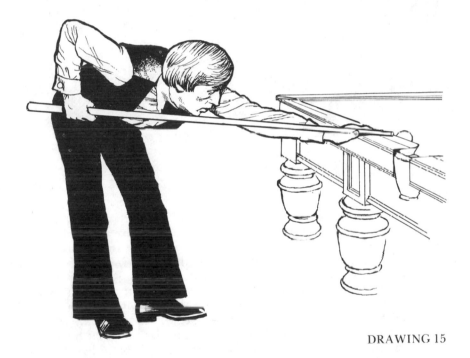

DRAWING 15

much power with a short bridge because you cannot draw the cue back far enough to hit the cue-ball as hard as you need.

When the cue-ball is just off the cushion, many players favour the loop bridge with the cue running underneath the first and second fingers (drawing 16 – see next page). I have never felt happy with this bridge and have always used basically the same bridge as the one I use for playing from under the cushion. The drawing shows quite a dis-

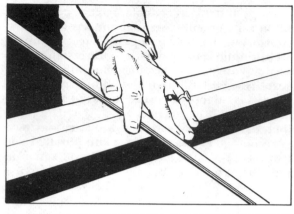

DRAWING 16

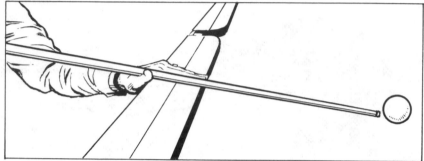

DRAWING 17

tance from bridge to cue-ball. I would be holding my cue right at the very end for this shot but would shorten my grip if the cue-ball was nearer the cushion. If the cue-ball was further out I would, of course, be able to place my bridge on the table bed.

All other things being equal, the taller the player, the more he is at a disadvantage if he is playing from under the cushion because he has that much further to bend. A notable exception to this rule is John Spencer, who is six foot tall but so supple in the hips that he always seems to get down to this sort of shot very comfortably. Alwyn Lloyd, who has won the Welsh Amateur Championship three times and who is only about 5 feet 6 inches, actually prefers playing with his bridge hand on the cushion rail with the cue-ball a few inches out from it. He is less happy when the cue-ball gets well out into the middle of the table when he has to get more of his body above table level.

The rules stipulate that the table shall be between 2 feet 9½ inches and 2 feet 10½ inches from the floor. That inch can be quite important. The tables for the 1974 World Professional Championship were as high as the rules permitted and to make matters worse for the shorter players, the floor was uneven enough to give the impression that in certain places you were standing in a hole. Fred Davis, battling all the time against the feeling that the table was too high for him, skinned the knuckles of his cue hand through persistently catching them on the cushion rail on his follow-through. His action had become so grooved over the years that even with his vast experience he could not adjust it.

Basically, I use two methods for bridging over a ball. When there is a fair distance between the obstructing ball and the cue-ball (drawing 18, top) I tend to bridge with the fingers closed, the top knuckles raised as high as possible and the heel of the hand touching the table. I am thus supporting my bridge in two ways.

When there is very little distance between the two balls (drawing 18, bottom), the butt of the cue has to be elevated much more to avoid fouling the obstructing ball as it strikes downwards at the cue-ball. In this situation, I spread the fingers more widely, pressing them firmly into the bed of the table for maximum stability. There are two fingers in a forward position and two back. The cue is kept on line between the thumb and top knuckle of the first finger.

As the distance between obstructing ball and cue-ball decreases, so the cue's angle of elevation needs to rise. The steeper the angle, the

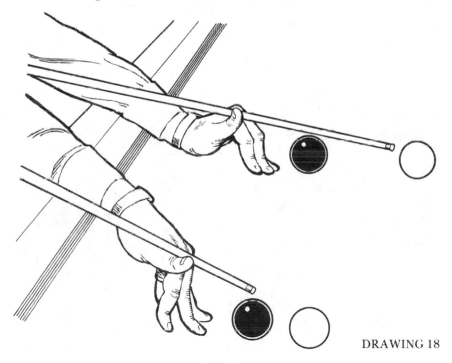

DRAWING 18

more the body tends to arch into the shot, often demanding that the player stands on tiptoe on his back (right) foot. As this happens, so the grip on the butt of the cue progressively shortens.

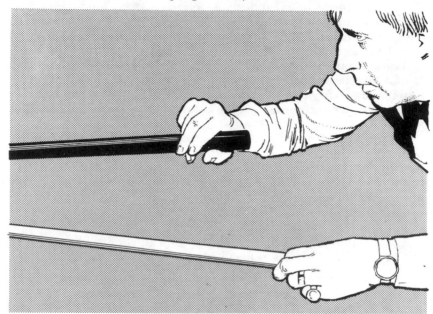

DRAWING 19

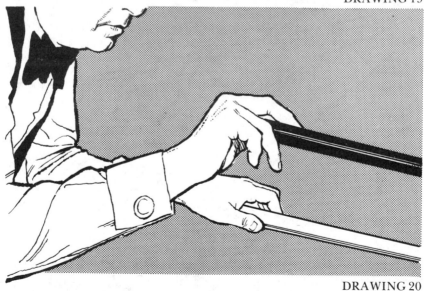

DRAWING 20

## USING THE REST

When using the rest, the elbow is not behind the cue as it is ordinarily but at the side. The cue therefore has to be thrust through with a sideways motion.

The cue is cradled by my thumb (drawings 19 and 20). It has a little support from my third finger on the opposite side of the cue but not much. My first and second fingers are lightly gripping the side of the cue above my thumb. Some players actually get most of the hand behind the butt of the cue but this style does not suit me.

The purists might say that my right elbow is a little low (drawing 21 – see below). Ray Reardon, who is as good with the rest as anybody

DRAWING 21

has ever been, has his lower right arm horizontal. Again, there is a school of thought which believes that the rest itself should be running directly underneath the cue but this feels cramped to me. One of the advantages in placing the rest at an angle as I do is that it enables me to distribute my body weight more widely and evenly than would be possible if my left hand was holding the rest on the table underneath

DRAWING 22

my chin. I don't think it is necessary to place your left hand on top of the rest. You can keep it perfectly still, which is all that matters, with a light finger grip.

With the normal hand bridge you have the advantage of your cue being kept on line by brushing lightly against your chest. The lack of this aid is one reason why most players find it more difficult to deliver the cue through straight when using the rest. It is very important indeed to keep the body perfectly still as you thrust the cue through.

Until I started work on this book, I did not realise how important my stance (drawing 22 – see left page) was in this respect. You will notice that my left foot is pointing away at right angles while my right foot is pointing straight ahead. My back is therefore slightly twisted to the line of the shot rather than straight behind it. This helps me get sideways, rather like a tennis player playing a backhand.

DRAWING 23

I always use the rest 'short way up' unless I am playing a shot which requires me to strike the cue-ball well above centre. If you use it 'tall way up' for other shots you will find yourself digging down at the cue-ball and increasing the risk of swerving the ball unintentionally. One situation in which this is unavoidable is when you have to use the spider (drawing 23 – see left page). The butt has to be elevated so I have to stand up not all that far short of my full height to play the shot. My body tends to be more directly behind the cue than it is when I use the ordinary rest. Your range of shots is very limited with the spider, your chances of success being greatest with the shortest of backswings and not much follow-through. It is futile to be at all ambitious with this implement.

# 4

# Early Days:
# My Amateur Career

Until I started playing snooker, I was a proper little tearaway, always in trouble. One night, when I was eleven, a policeman caught us breaking into a groundsman's shed to get a drink of pop. I was put on probation. You can write this and all our other escapades off to high spirits now, but I'm convinced I would eventually have landed myself in deep trouble if it had not been for snooker. When I started playing, at fourteen, I changed very quickly. Instead of roaming about in a gang I became much more of a loner.

I passed my eleven plus, but after a year at Llanelli Grammar School I was expelled for 'widging' – truancy. Instead of going to school, I'd go to the park. My dad gave me a hiding but it made no difference. I wouldn't go back. I had it in my head that they were all snobs at grammar school. All my friends were at the secondary modern.

At the time it never sank in how poorly off our family was. My father was a steelworker. My mother, who had had trouble with her legs as long as I can remember, had various jobs as well and it was hard going for them bringing up the three of us – my sister Lynn, who is six years older than me, my brother Barrie, who is three years older, and myself. I was a teenager before I had my first suit.

None of this bothered me then or now. Looking back, it was a happy home – but at the time I never stopped to think whether it was or not. It was just home. I played all sports, mostly cricket and soccer in the park. I was never all that keen on rugby, but we had to play it at school.

Barry Llewellyn, who went on to become a Welsh international, was in the first year team with me at grammar school, and at secondary modern I was in the same team as Phil Bennett, Derek Quinnell, quite a few others who went on to play for Llanelli, and Brian Butler and Eric Watts, who eventually played rugby league.

Phil was always outstanding. When he was twelve he was playing for the fifteen and overs and he was already one of the best players in the team. He was just as good at soccer and cricket. Derek wasn't outstanding. You wouldn't have looked at him and seen a future Welsh international and British Lion. He didn't even look all that big. His success has come from a lot of hard work, dedication and perseverance.

Our team was the best in the area by such a margin that when it came to the Llanelli Schools representative team trial we were selected *en bloc* as one team, including me at full-back. That was by far the easiest position in the team. All I had to do was to run back and forth behind the centres. Full-backs didn't come into the line in those days. The gym master gave you a hiding if you did.

The school rugby team, 1961-62. I am second from the right in the back row, while Welsh rugby international Phil Bennett is sitting in the front row, far right.

At fifteen, I went into the mines. The pay was £6 a week, when apprentices were getting thirty bob. You worked on the surface first, then went underground. I trained as a welder, then I went into the blacksmith's shop to train as a striker. I had to get up at five to catch the five-forty bus. I was at the colliery by seven, home by four. I always had blisters on my hands and I was always in bed early because I was so tired. It was very hard work. What made it bearable and even enjoyable were the people I worked with and the people I met.

My brother was a bus conductor and after three years I went on the buses too. It was £14 a week, plus overtime; big money it seemed, and enjoyable because I was amongst people all the time. I met my wife, Annette, on a bus, and a combination of starting courting and working shifts led to me packing up snooker for a whole season. I missed it so badly that I weakened towards the end of the season and played a few games.

Since I had started playing, I had improved steadily just through playing. I had no great ambition, no great dreams, even though within my own range I was very competitive. I played for various teams in the Llanelli and District League and it amazes me now to think that I arranged my whole week round one frame of league snooker on a Wednesday night. If we had an away match in Ammanford, which is only 15 miles, I would arrange my shifts so that I could lie in next morning. A match followed by a lie in was something to look forward to. That one frame of league snooker was turned over and over in my mind, endlessly, particularly if I had lost – far more than I would ever do now. In those days, I couldn't stop thinking of the shots I had missed, whereas now I can accept more easily that everyone misses shots. You were trying to pot them at the time and you missed. OK. Accept it. Don't keep going over old ground. Just try your hardest next time.

I remember my improvement chiefly by the breaks I made. In my first year of playing I made a 33, but went home one night about a year later thrilled to bits at making a 48. I broke the 50 barrier with a 53 and increased my best quite regularly until I stuck for a long time on 75. I was twenty-four before I made my first century, though I still thought of a 90 I made in the West Wales Championship as my best.

The best players around Llanelli at that time were Len Jones, who couldn't pot as well as I could but who used to beat me on safety and tactics, and Peter Davies, who always seemed to raise his game at the colours stage. Peter had a way of going for his shots very positively on the colours and much more often than not he used to get them. I am sure this is the best way to play.

From the start I seemed to pot a ball reasonably well, but it didn't really dawn on me how much there was to the game until I went to see Mario Berni play when I was sixteen. Mario was Welsh amateur champion in 1964 but his reputation is founded not so much on what he has achieved as a player as on his vast knowledge of the technique and mechanics of the game. 'The Professor' knows just about everything there is to know about the game, but it has perhaps been his undoing that he has tried to play perfectly rather than make winning his primary aim. You need to be roughly aware how you play certain shots but if you look inwards too much you tend to put pressure on yourself rather than on your opponent. This is what has often happened to Mario though he has remained a first-class player and, for me, a very good practice opponent. I had several sessions with him at his club, the Mackworth in Neath, just before the world championship and these proved to be just the sort of preparation I needed.

Between 1956 and 1969 there was no professional snooker to speak of: no television, no press coverage, very little opportunity to see good players from other parts of the country. Down in West Wales we were out on a limb and didn't even venture into South Wales much. Neath, where Mario was based, was about the edge of the snooker world as far as I was concerned.

Another Mackworth boy, Jim Selby, who also became a Welsh international, was my opponent in the West Wales final when I was seventeen. In the first frame, he was 26 in front on the green. I gave him a snooker which was very easy to hit, but which somehow he missed, and it struck me that although he was a much better player than I was at the time he was perhaps feeling a bit of pressure. He fell apart after this and I won 4-0. It was nice to win, and I also realised that I could play to the same standard in matches that I could in practice. Not everyone can do that.

I didn't get carried away, didn't think of this success as leading to anything in particular, any more than I did when I won the Llanelli and District Championship, which was played on a handicap basis anyway. From conversations I've had in the last year it seems that I didn't fantasise when I was younger as much as many players seem to have done. I can honestly say that I never had visions of being world champion, of being a professional even, until these things were obviously achievable.

At that time, my snooker life carried on very much as it had before. I played because I liked playing, sticking to my natural style but making a couple of small adjustments when I could see these as a way to improve. The most important of these was in my bridge, which I changed for reasons I went into fully in Chapter 3.

After two years on the buses I became a postman. Not only did this pay more money, the prime consideration, at £18 per week plus overtime, but it was a better career. There was also an easier shift system, which meant that I could go straight from work to play snooker in the afternoons. I can remember starting to think more about the game at this time, and I also went through a phase of playing a lot of safety. It was good that I should find out more about this side of the game though if you don't watch it you can slip into the habit of regarding safety as an end in itself: and then you can lose sight of the fact that at some stage you have to pot the balls to win.

I got married in 1969: I was twenty-one and Annette nineteen. I saw London for the first time on my honeymoon. Prior to that I had hardly been anywhere. Even a trip to Cardiff train spotting when I was very young stood out as something special. My elder son, Wayne, was born in 1971 and Darren in 1973.

In the summer of 1971, my mother died. She had been ill for years, in and out of hospital several times, and when she went into hospital again, it never dawned on me that she might die. When she did, it hit me, particularly in making me feel guilty that I hadn't done enough for her when she was alive. I think I treat my father better because of it, though we've always been close and he has always enjoyed coming to my matches. Some of my successes have made him very emotional and of course his pleasure contributes to my own.

The family at home – from left to right, Darren, myself, Annette and Wayne.

In the 1971-72 season, I entered the Welsh Amateur Championship for the first time. I had been to see quite a few matches so I didn't expect to get knocked off the table but, even so, I wouldn't have been surprised to lose early on. As it was, I reached the final, beating Dilwyn John (who used to keep goal for Cardiff City) 4-2 to get there.

At this point, everyone assured me that I was a certainty. Having been told that I was going to win, I *had* won in my mind – so when I was 4-0 down at the interval against Geoff Thomas in the final I felt crushed. Even though it was best of eleven, I knew I had lost. Keith Robinson, one of the Welsh officials (who has always gone out of his way to help me) very tactfully mentioned during the interval that in the event of an early finish I would be expected to play a couple more frames in order to give ticket holders their money's-worth. Instead of feeling insulted this made me feel a lot better. I'd forgotten about winning but I desperately wanted to produce some form which would show that I could play a bit. With at least two more match frames and two exhibition frames I would have four chances.

In the evening session, I was much more relaxed. I made it 2-4 and if I hadn't missed an easy red in the middle pocket with a good break on, it would have been 3-4. I was too inexperienced at the time to realise how much I had Geoff under pressure. If it had been 3-4, anything could have happened – but Geoff won this frame and the next, to win 6-2.

I lost because I still didn't know how to play a match. I could pot well, I could screw a ball, I could do a bit of most things, but I didn't know how to blend it all into a match-winning pattern. Geoff didn't look all that much but he didn't miss when he was in and at the first sign of trouble he played safe. He was also a very good finisher. Time and again he would knock in the last two or three reds and all the colours if you gave him half a chance.

That match was very important to me because I was able to accept defeat within myself for the first time. Previously, I wouldn't have slept. I realised that I had expected too much and that I hadn't learnt to respect sufficiently the players whose results proved they were better than they appeared.

One result of reaching this Welsh final was that I was picked a few times as reserve for Wales in international matches, playing an exhibition frame against the opposition's reserve before each session. I had been told that I was certain to be in the team so I was disappointed when Mal Hendra, the team manager, took me aside to say: 'We feel you need a bit more experience.'

'What sort of experience? I've been playing for years', I felt like saying, but they were right. In my first match as an international reserve I couldn't hold my cue steady. As reserve, though, I was able to absorb the atmosphere of internationals without being put under the pressure of having to win. I came into the team for the last two matches of the 1973-74 season when I beat Pascal Burke 2-1 in Dublin and John Phillips 3-0 in Edinburgh.

In many ways, the pressure of playing team matches, particularly internationals, is greater than playing for oneself. It is very difficult to sit watching the early matches, very much involved in them, and then play. If you are not careful you can be emotionally drained before you even take your cue out of your case. Team experience was invaluable for me when professional snooker's first ever World Cup took place in 1979, and Doug Mountjoy, Ray Reardon and I won it for Wales.

The amateur internationals broadened my experience in other ways, too. There is a world of difference between living at home and just popping down the road to play a match, and travelling hundreds of miles to play far away from familiar surroundings and routine. Being with other Welsh players on the away trips, which was enjoyable in itself, helped me get to grips with these problems without me even realising that they were problems. I played fourteen times for Wales between 1973 and 1978 and only lost twice. The matches were six-a-side, each player playing three frames. I won thirty-three frames out of forty-two. We won the championship in 1974-75, 1975-76 and 1977-78.

My next small breakthrough was to win the Welsh area of the English Amateur Championship in 1974. This gave me the pleasure of a seven hours and fifty minutes drive from Llanelli to Chelmsford to play Vic Harris, who, as luck would have it, lived only a few miles away at Dagenham. My old car was hardly up to it; the traffic, as soon as we hit the outskirts of London, moved at a crawl and I was already shattered by the time I arrived, ten minutes before the match was due to start at three o'clock. I had left home at seven.

In no time I was two down, then led 3-2, but lost 4-3. 'When you were 3-2 up, I couldn't see how I could win', Vic said afterwards. This made me feel a bit better, but it was a very long drive home again.

In the autumn of 1974, I played on television for the first time in the first of what became an annual two-day tournament in HTV's studios in Cardiff. Playing on television doesn't bother me at all now but then I was terrified. In the semi-final against Mario Berni I had a very simple, almost straight pink, followed by a very simple black to win – but how I potted them I don't know. As I was lining the shots up, I was saying to myself: 'I'll never get this.' Nevertheless I went on to beat Dilwyn John in the final, and was then able to sit back and watch the series. This also made me realise how fat I looked. I was fifteen-and-a-half stone, so I more or less stopped eating. I lost one-and-a-half stone in two weeks and three-and-a-half stone in all. Since then, I haven't moved much from around the twelve-stone mark.

The experience of the HTV tournament, getting used to playing in front of cameras and seeing myself on the screen, was invaluable. Of the four years I played in it, I won it twice and lost in the final once.

I did nothing in the Welsh in 1973 and 1974, but I won in 1975 beating Geoff Thomas 8-7 in the final. Geoff had lost two Welsh finals and the 1974 World Amateur final in Dublin since beating me in 1972, and I felt before the match that this might put extra pressure on him if it was close. If a player loses a few close, important matches it tends to make him too eager to compensate when a similar situation recurs. At the back of his mind is the memory of how awful he felt when he just missed the boat. This makes him anxious to avoid similar mistakes, which is in itself a bad attitude – because he is thinking negatively about not losing, rather than positively about winning. He either becomes tentative, hoping his opponent will virtually give him the match, or so desperate to clinch it that he lunges out and hopes for the best.

When there is not all that much between players, it is what goes on in their minds which is usually decisive. This particular match was a strange one because we were both full of inhibitions. I didn't feel

An overweight Terry Griffiths makes his Welsh Amateur Championship debut, against John Terry, who also became a Welsh international.

nervous at the start – I think it would have been better if I had – but my cue arm felt so heavy in the first frame that I couldn't get back down the table with my safety shots. It was just as well that Geoff didn't leave me any chances because if I'd missed them it could have affected my confidence.

After losing that frame, my arm felt a bit looser, and I won the next three. Then people started to say I was going to be 6-1 up at the end of the first night's play, and that seemed to depress me. Geoff, who is a great fighter, usually a better player when he is down than when he's in front, won the remaining three frames on the first night to lead 4-3.

Going home in the car, I did feel very depressed. I felt I had produced some form but hadn't used it to best effect. A good opportunity to take a commanding lead had been wasted but I got over this feeling by the time we started on the second night.

I made it 4-4 and levelled again at 5-5, but lost the next after Geoff had needed a snooker with only the pink and black left. This is the sort of frame which, psychologically, can decide a match. The player who has lost it feels so furious with himself that it can enter his mind that he doesn't deserve to win. For the player who has won the frame it is like, in a small way, having looked death in the face and got away with it. It generally gives him a new charge of energy and confidence, and this is what happened this time. Geoff won the twelfth frame as well, to lead 7-5, two up with three to play.

Now Geoff was so nearly past the post that in his mind he had everything to lose. The disappointment of losing is all the greater when you know you should have won.

My own position was that I was facing defeat. I had to acknowledge that it was likely that I would lose. Once I had done that, I had, in a sense, nothing *to* lose. I made a 76 break to make it 6-7. In the next frame, I felt that the run of the balls, which had favoured Geoff earlier, was starting to favour me. Irrational as it may be, a player only has to have a couple of friendly rubs of the green at the right time for him to feel that the gods are prepared to give him a little help if he holds his game together. Geoff, on the other hand, as these rubs started to go against him at this stage, may well have felt that the gods were all set to give him another smack in the face.

When I made it 7-7, I felt there was no way I could lose the decider. I had built up so much momentum that I felt that if Geoff left me a ball on anywhere I was going to pot it. The frame wasn't decided until the colours, but at no time did I think I would lose it.

On the strength of this victory, the Welsh Billiards and Snooker Association decided, about six months later, that I would be one of the two Welsh representatives in the World Amateur Snooker Championship in Johannesburg. The winner of the 1976 Welsh title would be the other. It was just as well that selection did not depend on my performances in the 1976 season. I was starting to have problems with my game and over the winter my confidence dwindled to zero. Had I not known I was going to South Africa I might have packed up snooker altogether.

The root of my problems was my cue. It kept splitting near the tip, and to keep the same length I had to cut bits off the top and extend it at the bottom. This altered the balance, and in the end I had to give up. The weight of the cue had increased from 16 ounces to 20, and the butt had become very thick. I tried several others, but it was a long time before one felt right. It is the one I still use – 16 ounces with a very slim butt.

I had another change of job from postman to insurance agent with the Pearl Insurance Company. The main attractions were more money and more flexible hours, but the job was also very good for me in that it brought me out and made me a lot more confident in meeting and talking to people.

In the Welsh, I lost 4-1 in the last sixteen to Dai Thomas, who later came within one ball of beating Doug Mountjoy in the semi. Dai had only to pot the blue with the rest to win 7-5, but twice had to get up from his shot because a moth settled on the ball. This probably upset his concentration because he missed the blue when he got down for a third time. Doug went on to win 7-6 and then beat Alwyn Lloyd in the final to earn the trip to South Africa as reigning Welsh champion. From there, he won the World Amateur which, when he turned professional, earned him an immediate invitation into the Benson and Hedges Masters, which he also won. If you believe in fate, it was fate that chose that particular moment for the moth to settle on the blue!

Doug Mountjoy and I in South Africa for the 1976 World Amateur.

On the other hand, if you believe that fate helps those who deserve it, that was also true. In 1974, Doug had become the first amateur to win a £1,000 prize when he won the first Pontins Open at Prestatyn. About the same time he found himself out of work, so he really buckled down to his snooker with a view to turning professional. He had made up his mind that he was going to do so in November 1976, so he was very keen to finish his amateur career in a blaze of glory – not just for his personal satisfaction but because amateur titles are indirectly, in those circumstances, financial assets.

Doug was playing marvellously in practice and in most matches, too, but against Dai the pressure caught up with him. Winning meant too much to him, so much that he was playing not to lose instead of to win. He would not have won if he had not had a slice of luck at the right time.

Once Doug had won the Welsh title, he was a strong favourite for the World Amateur which was played over three long weeks in the five-star President Hotel in Johannesburg. It was the first time I had been abroad, and the first time I had been away from home for anything like three weeks. The match tables were first-class and the tournament was exceptionally well organised but after a week I was thoroughly homesick. I felt out of touch with myself and my game just fell apart.

The field was divided into three round-robin groups, with three from each qualifying for the knock-out stages. Two of the three third place finishers had to play the 'extra' match to reduce the field to eight.

Three wins, 4-0, 4-0 and 4-1, got me away well but the rot set in when I lost to one of the South Africans, Silvino Francisco, 4-2. Having trailed 0-3, which funnily enough was the only time I felt I could win, I nearly made it 3-3 but left the pink over the pocket when I made an all-or-nothing attempt at it down the side rail. After losing this match quite late at night, I had not recovered by the time I played Paul Mifsud, the Malta champion, at 9am next morning. I could not rate Paul very highly but my cueing was all over the place and I lost easily 4-1. This meant that I had to win my last two matches to qualify.

The first of these, against the Canadian, Bob Paquette, was one of the most amazing I have ever played. I led 2-0 and 3-2, and in a tense finish to the sixth frame cut the pink in for match, length of the table, only to go in-off in a baulk pocket. This also meant that Bob, instead of needing two colours to win this frame for 3-3, needed only one. He attempted an easy pink at speed across the table – why he hit it so hard I don't know – only for it to hit the far jaw of the middle pocket and shoot off at an incredible right angle, hugging the cushion all the way to finish in the corner pocket.

The seventh frame, the decider, was equally desperate. Bob needed a snooker on the colours, got it, and took the colours up to the blue. He put me in trouble with a safety shot on the pink. I made a real hash of my safety shot but the pink crept into the baulk pocket at its last roll to give me the match. I then beat Eddie Swaffield of Northern Ireland 4-2 (on the black in the sixth) to finish third in my group.

Of the three third place finishers, Ray Edmonds drew the short straw so I had to play another English representative, Roy Andrewartha, for a place in the quarter-finals. Feeling more confident than I had been, I beat him 4-0 but then lost 5-3 to Jimmy van Rensburg in the quarters.

Jimmy, who lives just outside Johannesburg, had the advantage of leading a relatively normal life during the championship instead of having to endure the luxurious claustrophobia of the visiting competitors; consequently he was calm and steady while I was in and out. When I was 3-4 down I missed a ridiculously easy red in the middle pocket with a possible frame-winning break to follow. In the end, I potted a very good green but went in-off to give him an easy chance to take the few balls he needed. This was very unlucky, but the situation would never have arisen if I had not missed that easy chance earlier on. I fought hard, as I always do. But I wasn't surprised that I lost because, in my bones, I felt a loser, apprehensively nervous before I started instead of eagerly nervous as I like to be.

Once I had lost I felt further away from home than ever. Doug was going great guns and eventually won the championship easily, beating Mifsud 11-1 in the final. I supported him as much as I could, as he supported me in my matches, but once I was out of the tournament I was desperate to get home. When I did, I was full of big ambitions, much more so than I had been before. Having seen Doug win, my thoughts were on the next World Amateur in Malta two years later. However, I lost 4-2 to Cliff Wilson in the quarter-final of the Welsh Amateur in 1977, which meant that I had to win it in 1978 to qualify. As it turned out, I was beaten 4-0 by Steve Newbury in the last sixteen, so I never played in the World Amateur again.

The curious thing is that if I'd won the Welsh in 1977 or 1978, I would certainly have gone to Malta in 1978, and I would not have turned professional until December 1978 at the earliest. In all probability I would not then have entered, let alone won, the World Professional Championship in April 1979.

What I did have to show for my last two years as an amateur, though, were two English Amateur Championships. That may sound strange for a Welshman, but entries for the 'English' are traditionally accepted from Wales and Scotland as well as England. Next to the World Amateur, it carries more weight than any other amateur title.

First I had to win the Welsh qualifying area, and then it was a 400-mile round trip for me every time I played at Fishers, Acton, in 1975 and 1976 in the Southern competition proper. I was entitled to second-class return rail fare but my actual expenses were much more. I didn't have the money for hotels, so I had to drive up, play, and drive back in the same day. In 1977, which was the first year I won it, I had to stay because my matches followed each other very quickly towards the end. I shared an attic with my father near Ealing Common, at £2 a night.

Patsy Fagan, who had reached the final in 1974, was a hot favourite in 1975. He was playing full-time in tournaments and money matches and his two managers, first Peter Careswell, then George Jackson, organised him so thoroughly that he only had his snooker to think about. He had a crowd of supporters who had a lot to say, so his matches had plenty of atmosphere. This didn't bother me – in fact there was more pressure on Patsy because his supporters expected him to win – and I beat him 4-1.

Patsy turned professional after the 1976 English Championship when he lost to Chris Ross in the Southern final after he had again been a very strong favourite. He won the first UK Professional Championship at Blackpool in 1977 and another tournament at Wembley Conference Centre, beating John Spencer and Alex Higgins. He won the last three frames to beat Alex Higgins 13-12 in the first round of the 1978 World Championship, but shortly after that he started having problems. The worst of these by far was in using the rest. He had been very good with it, in fact there wasn't much wrong with his game at all, but suddenly found that he could not thrust his cue through to hit the cue-ball on a rest shot. The ball he was trying to pot might be hanging over the pocket but it was still no good: no matter how he strained Patsy couldn't bring the cue through. Sometimes, he would break through this blockage in his co-ordination and manage to hit the cue-ball – not with any control, but at least he had hit it. Other times he just had to give up and play some other shot for which he didn't need the rest, perhaps playing off the cushion or playing what he knew was the wrong shot.

Patsy had to endure all this in front of millions of television viewers in the 1979 World Cup. It was agonising to watch, but it must have been a lot worse for him. He tried hypnosis, he tried lots of things, but he just had to live with the problem until, gradually, it started to trouble him less. There's no doubt though that this set him back very badly: from being up amongst the best in late 1977 and early 1978 it wasn't long before he was fighting for survival. That just shows you how uncertain snooker can be.

After beating Patsy, I led Willie Thorne 4-2 in the semi-final and lost 5-4. It was the first year that Willie had come really good. His style is very natural and fluent and he is always liable to have an inspired burst for three or four frames. Our match could have gone either way but once he had won it and beaten Chris Ross in the Southern final, most people expected him to beat Sid Hood, who had won the Northern section, in the national final.

Sid is a very experienced battler, not the sort to be underestimated, but if Willie had played to his potential he should have won. He lost and in a way this has been the story of his life so far. In the 1978 World Championship he lost to Eddie Charlton after being three up with four to play; in 1979 he lost 9-8 to John Virgo after leading 8-5; and in 1980 he lost 10-9 to Bill Werbeniuk. With all his ability he should have won more than he has but if you get into a pattern early in your professional career of losing close matches – as Willie has – it can be difficult to change it.

In 1976 I lost 4-3 on the final black to Geoff Foulds, a very sound and steady Londoner, very experienced, just the sort with whom you don't want to be drawn into a long match. It didn't help that I broke down on the motorway. The cylinder head gasket had blown, I had to rush to get to the match in time, and I had to come home on the train. I got straight off it to play for Llanelli against Cardiff in the Welsh Inter-Town Championship. After all this, I was fuming. 'That's the last time I play in the English', I said, but the next season there I was again.

Everything went very smoothly at first. I won the Southern for the loss of only two frames in four matches but four days before I was due to play Sid Hood in the English final at Romford I couldn't get out of bed with lumbago. Two days before the final I could only play standing half-upright and although I was determined to play as long as I could stand up, I was very depressed. Then I went to a physiotherapist at the Trostre Steelworks. He put his thumb in my back, I felt something move, and next day I was more or less all right.

When I got to Romford, I hit the balls about on the match table for half-an-hour – I hadn't played for a week – and started. After all this, I hardly missed a ball, finishing off with breaks of 89 and 88 in the last two frames and winning with a session to spare.

A few weeks later, I won £500 as runner-up in the Pontins Open at Prestatyn. This is one of the highlights of the snooker year as about 700 amateurs, many of them, like me, with their families, make Pontins into a snooker village for the week. The amateurs start off in the camp's billiard room upstairs playing a knock-out tournament in which matches are decided on the aggregate score of two frames. With such short matches, luck plays a big part, but if an amateur manages to reach the last twenty-four he goes into the hat with eight invited professionals in the last thirty-two where the matches are the best of seven frames.

The professionals then conceded 25 points in each frame which in my opinion should be too severe a handicap against top amateur opposition. (Now it is 30.) With this 25, I beat Cliff Thorburn 4-2, Eddie Charlton 4-1, Perrie Mans 4-3 and Dennis Taylor 4-1 to reach the final, but it gave me little satisfaction. With such a big start I felt that I wouldn't be able to forgive myself if I lost. If I'd been playing those players level I would have been looking for just one chance to get in and make a break to win the game. With 25 start, I was thinking all the time about not letting my opponents in. My defensive and tentative frame of mind was concentrated on the prize money rather than on playing the game as it should be played.

I tried hard to raise my game in the final against Alex Higgins, who was conceding me 21. He was not playing as an invited professional but had battled his way spectacularly through all the qualifying rounds. By the end of the week he had the crowd right behind him. It was 3-3 at the interval but he was well on top in the evening and won 7-4. There was £1,500 for him and £500 for me. It was enough to buy a lot of things we wanted at home and made me think that with the money coming into snooker there might be more where that came from.

For the first time, I started to consider seriously the implications of turning professional in the not-too-distant future. It may sound odd that I was able to pick up cash prizes as an amateur, but amateur regulations had been amended in 1972 to allow that. The World Professional Billiards and Snooker Association, which runs the professional game, restricts entry to events like the World Professional Championship, the United Kingdom Championship, the Benson and Hedges Masters and so on, to its own members. Applications for membership are considered by the committee, all of them leading players. In practice, this system means that amateurs are free to earn what they can from exhibitions and tournaments but they cannot enter the tournaments which carry really big money.

In my last couple of years as an amateur I travelled here, there and everywhere – from Southend in the south-east to Grimsby and Middlesbrough in the north – playing in invitation tournaments for leading amateurs, or events where the field also included some of the lesser known pros. One of these, the Greenall Whitley Open, was organised at a Warrington pub, the Royal Oak, by landlord Bill Rigby. Sid, the resident referee, was always accompanied by his dog, Patch, who slept under the scoreboard throughout all the matches. Once, I drove 320 miles to Middlesbrough, lost 4-3 on the final black to Jack Fitzmaurice and then drove 320 miles home, all in the same day.

Selling insurance as I did meant that I could arrange my working week around my playing commitments, but it was crossing my mind more and more often that I ould not want to go on leading this kind of life for ever. My ambitions were still focussed on the World Amateur but it was at the back of my mind that my lifestyle might have to change after that.

Although there were quite a few £100 and £200 prizes, the tournaments were very difficult to win and over a season, expenses swallowed up what you could earn. This meant that I had to settle down more and not travel so much, basically playing just within Wales, or else I had to find some way of making my snooker pay, which meant turning professional. I didn't want the life that went with being a professional – being away from home a lot, playing club exhibitions in strange towns – and Annette wasn't very keen on it either, though I knew she would always support whatever decision I eventually made. Without turning professional, I knew I could not put the time in to improve as a player. This is not just a matter of how many hours you practice but of how fresh and keen you are when you do. You can play to a reasonably high standard if you are working, and occasionally to a very high standard, but to play consistently at top level you need time to relax and build your whole life round your game.

Ambition didn't really come into it. I never thought of turning professional in order to become champion. The question was: if I turned professional, could I earn enough to be better off than I would have been otherwise?

When the time came to defend my English title I only just beat Tony Marsh, from Devon, 4-3 in the first round of the championship proper. Matches at that stage of the competition are now decided over 15 frames, which does slightly relieve the fear that a little-known player is going to play the game of his life and knock you out before you have got into your stride.

As it turned out, this was my only difficult match. In an all-Welsh Southern final, I beat Cliff Wilson 8-2, and a month later went on to beat Joe Johnson, the Northern champion, 13-6 at Blackpool to retain the title.

Cliff, who was already certain of going to Malta through winning the Welsh in 1977, was desperately keen to win the English but never did himself justice in our match. He has had two careers. In his youth, in the 1950s, he was the Hurricane Higgins of his day – very aggressive, very fast, no defence but such a good potter that he frightened most opponents before the match had hardly started. When Cliff and Ray Reardon both lived in Tredegar they had some great battles; but when Ray went to live at Stoke, Cliff lost interest and then developed eye trouble.

He started to play again in 1972. Although, by all accounts, he never consistently returned to his previous standard, he still had spells when he knocked everything in. Although his game looks crude in many ways, Cliff knows a lot about the mechanics of snooker. He can tell at a glance where a player is going wrong, and he has given me some useful advice from time to time. His wit is a bit sharp for some tastes, and I took a while to get over the night that he booked us to play at a club where the main attraction was the strippers who followed us . . .but I count Cliff as a friend.

In that Southern final, though, he couldn't do anything right. In one frame he mis-read the scoreboard. Thinking he was 28 behind on the colours he played a snooker when, in fact, he was only 26 behind and could have won by clearing the table. Then, in the last frame, when he only needed one ball to win, I played a foul stroke. Instead of playing the next shot himself, he asked me to go again. I knocked in a difficult red and won the frame on the black.

Full of confidence, I went to play Steve Newbury in the quarter-final of the Welsh Amateur three days later. Having used up my supply of nervous energy for the moment, I was very calm. It would have been better if I had more sense of danger because I couldn't pot a ball. The second and fourth frames were on the black, but almost before I realised what was happening the match was over. I had lost 4-0 so there was no trip to Malta for me. Cliff won the World Amateur and Alwyn Lloyd, who beat Steve 8-4 in the final of the Welsh Amateur, reached the quarters. I still had the English final against Joe Johnson to play but, once I had lost to Steve, I thought more and more about turning professional. After Malta, the next World Amateur was in Australia in 1980 and that seemed too far ahead. I applied for membership of the WPBSA and was accepted on 1 June, 1979.

# 5

# On the Threshold

Without the disappointments of my first few months as a professional I would never have won the world championship. The first of these, a 9-8 defeat by Rex Williams in the qualifying section of the United Kingdom Championship was the most crushing I have ever had. I was 8-2 up and lost seven frames in a row to go out. What it cost me in invitations and bookings I'll never know, but looking back I needed something like that to make me work harder.

Although I had been accepted as a professional on 1 June, I didn't pack my job in until the end of August. There was not much doing in the summer but to prepare for the winter I did practise a lot. By the time I came to play Rex in September I was playing really well and I was full of confidence. Too full.

Rex Williams, who gave me a traumatic start to my pro career.

When the draw was announced, I could see no reason why I shouldn't do well. Rex is a very experienced professional but he had not done much for several seasons. I could see myself getting through to the competition proper at Preston where I would have had to play Graham Miles, also very experienced, but again without much recent success. Another good omen was that Rex and I were playing at Romford Lucania, where I had never lost a match.

At the end of the afternoon session, I had won five games in a row to lead 6-2, but I was disappointed with the way I had played. Rex had got a few good shots but he had missed a number that he shouldn't have done and he was playing without much confidence.

At this stage, instead of being content just to win, I got it into my head that I had to shine as well. I won the first two frames at night to lead 8-2 – but still I wanted to finish with a big break.

After Rex had won the next frame, I had a position at 8-3 when, instead of waiting my chance, I again tried to win with a flourish. As diagram 5 shows, I was left with a very awkward green, cutting it back at about quarter-ball across and against the nap into the 'green' pocket.

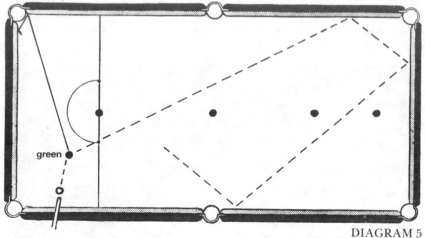

DIAGRAM 5

Playing with screw and right-hand side, I hoped to bring the cue-ball round off three cushions for the brown and clear up to win the frame.

It was a very dangerous shot, as I was more or less bound to leave the green if I missed it. Rex had still not found any form, so unless I left him easy chances the odds were very much in my favour. I could easily have played very thin off the green, hardly moving it, to take the cue-ball off the side cushion behind the black: or I could have screwed off the green with left-hand side to leave the cue-ball behind brown and blue and the green behind pink and black. As it was, I attempted the very risky pot and of course left the green over the pocket.

That was just the encouragement Rex needed. From 8-4 he started to play well, as a player often does when in his mind he has accepted that he has lost, only to find suddenly that he is still playing. If you accept you've lost, then you've nothing else to lose.

Even when I lost another frame, I didn't really see the danger signals. I still had to win only one frame out of four and there was no way, I thought, that I was not going to do that.

If I'm playing in a room which is just a bit sticky I keep washing my hands, sometimes after every frame, so that they feel clean and dry and my cue can run smoothly through my bridge. As I came out of the match room, I had to pass by the counter in the main room where Len Coates, the manager, kept an eye on all the tables in general use. As I passed him, at 8-2, 8-3, 8-4, and so on, we had the same conversation. He'd ask me the score, I'd tell him, and he'd say: 'It's OK, you'll win the next.' He was still saying that when the score was 8-8.

That was the first point at which I thought I could lose. It hit home how terrible it would be to lose after being so far in front, and I couldn't help regretting not making sure of winning before there was any real pressure and before Rex had got his tail up.

The picture had changed for Rex, too. He had been down and out, so everything good that happened to him, every frame he won, was a bonus. He had been trying hard and playing well to stay in the game, and now he had to change gear from mere survival to killing me off.

In the last frame he looked a lot more nervous that he had in the previous few. For different reasons, I was nervous as well, so it wasn't surprising that it came to a desperate finish. With pink and black left, Rex needed one ball and I needed two.

As diagram 6 shows, Rex had a good chance to pot the pink into the green pocket. If the shot had been the other side of the table it would

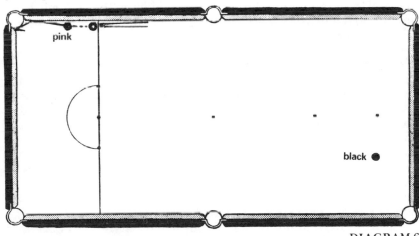

DIAGRAM 6

63

have been a certainty, as Rex would not have had to use the rest but, under pressure, a rest shot tends to feel slightly more difficult. Even so, with the pockets generously cut, I couldn't see him missing.

When he did, I shot out of my seat as if it was red hot. This, of course, was a sign of inexperience. I should have lingered a second or two, taken a deep breath, walked slowly to the table and done what I had to do. All my mind registered, though, was: 'I've got it.'

The pink was a very thin cut (diagram 7) but it looked quite straightforward to clip it in with a touch of left-hand side. Anywhere in the top part of the table, I thought, I was a certainty to pot the black.

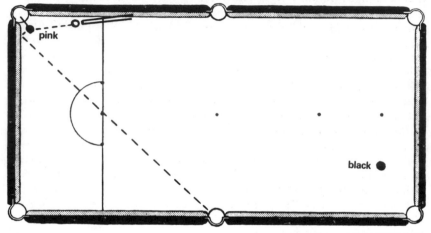

DIAGRAM 7

The next thing I knew, the cue-ball had flashed into the middle pocket. How it got there I don't know. I had played the pink much too hastily and not hit the cue-ball as I had intended. It would have been a miracle if I had won after that.

It takes a few hours for a failure like that to sink in. You go through the formalities, you shake hands, you try to raise a smile, you acknowledge, even if in your own mind you have thrown the match away, that your opponent deserves some credit too. I rang up Annette; I said a few words on the phone to BBC Wales who were interested in the match because it was, in effect, my professional debut; I tried to handle my disappointment as sportingly as I could. I think it helps if you can.

Next day, I was numb. I had three days exhibition bookings in Eastbourne, which I had been looking forward to because it was the first time, outside Wales, I had managed to string three bookings together. At last I felt I was on the road as a fully-fledged professional.

The drive from Romford to Eastbourne passed in a sort of trance. I stared blankly ahead, my head hardly moving one way or the other as if I had a stiff neck. I didn't want to think but, of course, I kept churning the match over and over in my mind. Losing was bad, but what was worse was that it meant that I had no chance of playing in any of the major invitation tournaments. I badly needed a good performance in the UK Championship because, outside snooker's hard-core followers, I was virtually unknown outside Wales. And if you're unknown how can you expect a club to book you?

Even in the last couple of years the professional scene has changed. There are more tournaments, so professionals, particularly the leading professionals, don't have to rely so much on exhibitions in the clubs. As one of the top amateurs, I could get £15 a night ... but not for very many nights. If I hadn't been seen quite a bit on HTV, I might not have had any at all.

When I turned professional, Jack Davies and Cyril Richards of Billiards and Snooker Wales, the table and equipment suppliers, helped me by distributing twelve hundred circulars to the clubs they serviced, but it was no good sitting back waiting for the bookings to roll in. Every Saturday and Sunday, I spent two or three hours on the phone chasing club secretaries, trying to drum up some shows.

A conversation might start:

'It's Terry Griffiths here. You've got a letter from me ...'

'Terry who?'

At another club I'd ask for the secretary:

'He's playing bingo. Ring back in half-an-hour.'

One or two told me straight out:

'We don't like snooker here.'

One secretary wouldn't be in, another would have gone home, and so it would go on. Annette would suddenly say something like: 'What about this electric bill?' Then I'd crash the phone down and give up.

For my first few months as a professional, I struggled to get two shows a week at £70 a time. One week I might have three, another none.

When I got to Eastbourne, John Hughes, Cyril Miles and the rest of the Eastbourne snooker crowd made me feel very welcome, but my losing to Rex didn't really register with them: understandably, because that had happened somewhere else and was not their immediate concern. But they were nice chaps, they had booked me, and I had a responsibility to pull myself together and put on a show worthy of my fee. I did my best, everyone seemed pleased enough, and by the end of the three days, the disappointment had eased a bit.

Unusually for me, I took a good three months to get over it properly. A few weeks later, I lost to Doug Mountjoy for the John Player Cup. I made a 104 break live on BBC Wales which couldn't have done me any harm but as soon as I lost a couple of frames all my confidence drained away.

I was practising very hard and, in practice, playing very well – but as soon as it came to a match my game went to nothing. This was hard to take as it had previously been the other way about. All my frustration erupted when I went back to Romford to play Graham Miles in the Lucania Pro-Am tournament and lost 5-3.

Graham was one of those professionals who, from a distance, had never looked all that good to me. He has this strange method of sighting with the cue not in the middle of his chin but almost under his left ear. If you stand behind him, his cue does not even seem to come through straight. His long potting, by professional standards, is relatively weak, but what I had not fully appreciated was how good his control is when he is 'in'. He has excellent touch in getting precisely the angle he wants in order to keep his break flowing smoothly and his breakmaking is very consistent. I discovered that he didn't miss or lose position once he was in, whereas I had been accustomed to even the best amateurs being less consistent in these ways.

Making every allowance for his strengths, I was still furious when I lost to Graham – not because I had lost but because I had not done myself justice. I amazed Barry Hearn, chairman of the Lucania chain of snooker clubs (who also manages Steve Davis), with my first – and so far, last – major outburst when I sat in his office after the match. He obviously thought that I wasn't capable of such an explosion!

In fact, Graham did very well in the UK that year, beating Rex 9-8 and Willie Thorne 9-1 with a break of 139, which is still the record for the event. He then lost 9-1 to Doug in the semi-final and Doug beat David Taylor 15-9 in the final. I went up to Preston to watch some of the tournament to taste the atmosphere. I think this helped me in my amateur days because not everything was strange and new when I came to be part of these events as a player. As I watched, I felt very disappointed that I was not competing but it did make me even more determined to make better use of my next chance.

Just before Christmas, I played in a tournament at the Castle Club, Southampton. The matches were short and the prize money not all that much but because the proprietor, Bernard Bennett, is a professional who is well liked in the snooker world, there was a good turn-out of professionals to support his tournament. What I was missing from my amateur days was regular matches. The idea of exhibitions is to go for everything and put on a show: winning isn't important as such. With matches you have to be prepared to play safe, striking the balance between being positive and taking mad risks. A completely different rhythm and mental approach is required.

I beat Geoff Foulds at Southampton, and then I beat Rex Williams 4-3 after leading 3-1. Rex again played very well when he was down and even in the deciding frame, after he had needed two snookers, he could have won on the colours. At the time, I didn't have the fear that history was going to repeat itself though, looking back, it obviously could have done. I potted a cracking yellow to put him back needing snookers again, went on to beat Bill Werbeniuk 4-1 and then lost 4-2 to Cliff Thorburn.

That tournament made me feel a lot better. I had been down as far as I could go, and now I felt I was on the up – though I didn't have a proper match between Christmas and March to test out my restored confidence. I knew in any case that everything depended on me getting through the qualifying section of the world championship and getting myself better known so that I could get more bookings. I had also made up my mind that if I lost in the qualifying, I would go back to work and be a part-time professional. It would be too frustrating, I thought, to know I had the ability and yet not get any results.

On top of this were financial pressures. You can't function as a professional unless you have a reliable car and a current driving licence. (Alex Higgins is an exception to this, as to every other rule.) The £136 a month I was then paying out for my Fiat was a lot of money. After the world championship in April, I had only two definite bookings, one at Bridgend, the other at Kilgetty, a village in Pembrokeshire. I was under a lot of pressure . . . but never felt it.

Bernard Bennett was my first opponent in the world qualifying at Romiley Forum, Stockport. I could not see myself having any trouble and didn't worry even when I lost the first two frames. There is a limit to the number of times you can prepare yourself to a fine edge and it is pointless to burn up any reserves to do so when it is not necessary. I was sure that my ordinary, average, or even below-average, game would be good enough and once I got my eye in the frames went pretty much one way. I won 9-2.

---

1979 World Championship
*Preliminary Round*
Griffiths beat Bernard Bennett 9-2
37-70;   48-73;   75(41)-16;   108(80)-9;   71-34(32);   97-9;
98(54)-13; 107-22; 89-31; 79-13; 74-44

---

I knew my task would be much harder against my second opponent, Jim Meadowcroft, who is not very well known to the general public but who is respected within the snooker world as a very useful performer. Jim turned professional in 1972 with no amateur successes to speak of – in fact the World Professional Billiards and Snooker Association wouldn't accept anyone as a professional now with such a slim record – and for years he always seemed to get a rough draw in the big events. He got to the world quarter-finals in 1976 and in 1977 he beat Ray Reardon in the UK Championship but, in general, the years slipped by without him making real impact.

1979 World Championship
*Qualifying Round*
Griffiths beat Jim Meadowcroft 9-6
53(35)-54;   109(52)-21;   88(30)-23;   65(52)-64(61);   24-72;
33-91(61);   109(91)-13;   99-23;   8-77(62);   69-66;
33(33)-100(56); 52-72; 53-38; 86-14; 64(38)-8

Jim was desperate to qualify for the championship proper in Sheffield – as I was – and in the first qualifying round he had done well to beat Jimmy van Rensburg, who had beaten me in the world amateur quarter-finals in 1976. Against me, Jim won the first frame on the black, the only time he was in front, but he levelled at 3-3 after I had led 3-1 and almost did so again at 5-5 after I had led 5-3.

At 5-4, I won a very important frame on the black – there's a very big difference between 5-5 and 6-4 – in which the crucial shot was a pink which Jim turned down at the end of this frame (see diagram 8). He had potted a few balls so he was in his stride. He had a long pink for

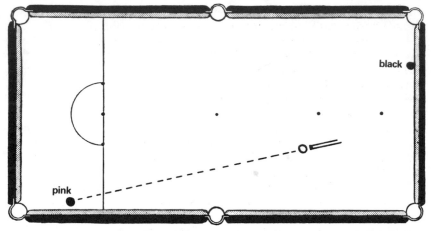

DIAGRAM 8

game, the pink only just off the side rail but very pottable because the pockets were generous to balls down the cushion. Jim refused it in favour of a safety shot. If winning hadn't been so important to him he would probably have gone for it and got it; but he couldn't bring himself to take such an important risk and, as it turned out, he never had a better chance. He battled back again from 4-6 to 6-6, but never had the initiative. The thirteenth frame was close but once I'd won it on the pink, Jim faded out.

The difference between us was that I had had an amateur career which had given me the experience of playing matches – and often winning them – under pressure. Once you have been used to doing that you know you can do it again. But Jim had had no substantial amateur record, and a professional career which had consisted mostly of giving a good account of himself against better known players but still losing. The longer this goes on the more the mind creates a barrier to winning when it really matters.

By qualifying, I was sure of £1,000, which meant that I could pay off what I owed on the car. Having seen a lot of the championship on television the previous year, I was excited by the thought of playing at the Crucible and for the first time being part of a big professional event. Losing to Rex Williams in the UK qualifying tournament had knocked me back but had made me work harder. The benefit was coming through now. I could feel everything within me knitting together: things were coming good.

This was not just because of snooker. In my experience, the game very rarely goes right for you if you have any worries about the really basic elements of life: home, family, health . . . and money. Not piles of it, but enough for the standard of life you have set for yourself and your family.

Some players can shut everything except snooker out of their minds. There are times when I have to try to do this myself. But the players who do it all the time put pressure on themselves by making the game too important. If it's virtually the only thing in your life that matters, the internal pressure on you to win is all the greater: if you lose, there's nothing left. I don't like losing either and a few defeats have gone deep – but these have only seemed like the end of the world until I have got home.

With no immediate worries, I felt as if I had everything to gain and nothing to lose. The draw for the championship proper had put me against Perrie Mans, who had reached the final the previous year but who was very beatable, I felt. By coincidence I had got him four exhibition bookings with me in West Wales just after Christmas. I was not a big enough name to get many bookings on my own but there were clubs who were prepared to book me if I could bring along one of the players they were used to seeing in the big televised tournaments.

You can't tell much from the results of exhibition matches but Perrie showed nothing in his range of shots or the way he played on those four nights to make me think I was the underdog the public thought I was. A few people in the snooker world told me that they fancied my chances against him, but it slightly reduced the pressure on me that the public as a whole expected him to beat me.

WORLD PROFESSIONAL SNOOKER CHAMPION 1979

# 6

# A Fortnight at the Crucible

I had never set foot in the Crucible Theatre before I walked into it for my first match. This was unusual as I had made a point of going along as a spectator to events I anticipated that I might later play in. In my early days, I attended the Welsh amateur championship; later in my amateur career I spent a couple of days watching the Benson and Hedges Masters. Usually it has turned out to be time well spent. I am very sensitive to atmosphere and I like to know what to expect.

I was tense at the start and missed an easy black which put me 2-1 down, but once I had settled I played well to lead 6-2 at the first interval. In the evening session my inexperience found me out: I started to tire, not physically but with the mental effort of having to concentrate for so long. Only against Rex Williams in the UK qualifying tournament six months previously had I ever played 17 frames in one day.

After winning a frame on the black for 8-2, I lost two of the next three. Then Perrie led 62-0 in the next but I cleared up with 63 to lead 10-4. In my mind, 10 was a special target, perhaps because once I was in double figures I was within sight of winning. So this was a vital frame to win. If the score had been only 9-5 I could have been struggling, because I then lost the last three frames of the day. Perrie, with his much greater experience, was well aware that if he could only hang on he still had a chance.

---

1979 World Championship
*First Round*
Griffiths beat Perrie Mans 13-8
I  72-23;  16-60;  47-54;  64-42;  69-20;  126(35,87)-9;
60(32)-50; 73(33)-31 (Griffiths 6-2)
II  103(40)-19;  79(46)-75(38);  25-74(34,34);  83(35)-41;
28-59; 63(63)-62(30); 27-92(43); 35-68; 36-71 (Griffiths 10-7)
III  43(39)-77(39); 83(56)-12; 81(46)-21; 70(38)-31

---

Overnight, I led 10-7, which was a lot more comfortable than 9-8 would have been, particularly as I lost the first frame the next day. But I felt fresh and rested, and from 10-8 won three in a row to win the match 13-8. It could have been – and was – described as a comfortable

71

victory but when you are playing it is never as comfortable as the final score might suggest.

Going out to play Alex Higgins in the quarter-finals I was very nervous, as it turned out with good reason. Alex played as well in the first session as he has ever played in a major tournament. He is so fast and can make the game look so easy that an opponent can become fascinated with what Alex is doing, so much so that when it comes to his own turn he can't play to his full ability. At least, while Alex was at the table, which was most of the time in the first session, I held on to my concentration.

I pinched the first frame on the black with a 61 clearance and then sat down while Alex made a break of 105 in the second frame and 112 in the third. In the fourth, he was well in with 45 and looking good for three centuries in a row, which would have been a championship record, when he missed unexpectedly.

The second and third frames had both gone by without me potting a ball and I'd only scored one in the fourth – but somehow my touch was still there when a chance came my way and I cleared up with 63 to win on the black. It was 2-2 at the mid-session interval and we'd been playing only 46 minutes.

Mid-session intervals often change the pattern of a match. Inspiration can peter out in the twenty minutes or so you are off the table or, if you are struggling, a quiet sit down with a cup of tea can get your mind and game together. I was hoping that Alex would go off the boil in the interval but he didn't. I didn't play badly but I couldn't hold him and it was 6-2 at the interval.

Psychologically, this was my lowest point in the championship. I was a long way behind and it seemed worse because Alex was playing so well. I didn't think about winning at this stage: I was far more concerned with not losing heavily. By the time we went back for the evening session I was determined just to hold on and do the best I could.

The first three frames went to the pink or black but I won them all to pull up to 5-6. He had won his six frames comfortably whereas my five had all been close ones. He had produced his best and still hadn't got clean away; I'd been struggling to hang on and yet I was only one behind. Then Alex surged again and got three in front; but I struck a purple patch in the last three frames of the day, making a 121 break in one and not giving him a look-in in the other two to reach 8-8 overnight. I was excited because after it had looked impossible earlier on, I now knew I could win.

Next morning, we swopped frame for frame. It was very good quality snooker with very little missed, but one mistake Alex did make was important. At 11-11, he was well in with 40, leading 55-0, when he missed a simple straight black from its spot. He had looked certain to go

---

1979 World Championship
*Quarter-finals*
Griffiths beat Alex Higgins 13-12
I   66(61)-55;   0-113(105);   0-134(112);   64(63)-59(45);
16-104(37,44);   24-100(39,44);   43(35)-75(45);   22-65(40)
(Higgins 6-2)
II   53(52)-48;   65(43)-55(35);   64-56;   30(30)-113(81);
28-77(37); 116-36; 127(121)-12; 118-0; (8-8)
III   70(35)-24;   47(46)-82(63);   33-86(32);   68(68)-31;
64(51)-46;   32(32)-109(61,32);   67(67)-55(40);   17-98(60,33);
107(107)-12

---

one up with two to play but when he missed I was able to clear up with 67 to win.

If you took away all the frames I won from behind in this match with 50 or 60 clearances, I would have lost quite easily. Winning them as I did showed that my nerve was good, always a useful thing to demonstrate to an opponent because it places all the more pressure on him to make the most of his chances.

Being one up with two to play instead of one down gave me just a little more margin of error. Alex won the next frame with a 60 but when I had a chance early in the decider I was able to take it with a break of 107.

This victory was very exciting for me, particularly when I could allow myself to relax and enjoy the thrill of such a success. I learnt afterwards that it had been agonising for Annette, though, who had been watching from the very back row of the theatre with Peter Francis, one of my oldest friends from Llanelli.

Annette had asked for time off work to come up to Sheffield to see me play and had been refused. She had packed up her job on the spot and came to Sheffield anyway, so when I did win the championship it was very nice that she didn't have to worry about finding another. This was all in the future though when she was watching me play Alex. Obviously she wanted me to win but she could sense as well that if I did our lives weren't going to be quite the same. Even if, on the face of it, you are going to be better off than you were before, there is part of you which is apprehensive about any major upheaval. So, with one thing and another, she could not bear to watch the whole match.

Peter has been a very loyal supporter. He paid his own fare, which took just about all he had at the time, to go to South Africa in 1976 to support me in the World Amateur, and he had helped me prepare for Sheffield by practising with me twice a day for two hours at a time – we couldn't get on the table for any more – at the Llanelli Conservative Club. He is a fair player, with a reasonable safety game, and he is quite capable of a 50 or 60 break. With a handicap, we can have a close, competitive game and he will always try his socks off to beat me. When I have been playing exceptionally well, the start I have been giving him has risen to a ridiculous amount, 60 or 70 sometimes. It is all part of the fun that whoever is getting the better of it should rub it in by any choice remarks that he can think of, so these occasions have tended to end with us playing in grim silence – Peter white-faced with determination to avoid losing with 70 start, me equally determined to have the sadistic pleasure of saying:'What's the matter with you? I'll have to give you 80 next time.'

In Sheffield, driving from the theatre to the hotel, either Peter or my father would say just the right thing. If things were going badly it was something to the effect that they could be worse or that I'd pick up next session. If they had gone well, it would be Peter usually who would recall some position I had made a hash of and bring me down to earth. This had happened all through my amateur career so, even though it was the world championship, the situation felt in this way the same as it always had. One of the keys to any success I've had has been to keep my everyday life as normal as possible so that a big occasion or anything out of the ordinary comes as an adventure. If you live at high pressure all the time you get used to it, but you also get dulled by it, so that you can't respond with anything extra when it is needed.

One journalist wrote that if playing Alex was like Russian roulette, playing Eddie Charlton was like the Battle of the Somme. With Alex frames are decided very quickly. He is a very good safety player but he will go for every half-chance and most quarter-chances. If you play the percentages against him, he is always likely to pull off a difficult shot and from it make a break which wins the frame. So you have to get in first or hope that when he does miss there are still enough balls left for you to win with a late run. It's kill or be killed.

Eddie's style represents the opposite extreme. He has a very straight cue action, pots very well, is very consistent and a very tough competitor. Against me, he was playing his sixth world semi-final in eight years. The fact that he had never won the title made this a doubtful advantage if it made him more anxious, as I think it did, not to let slip what must have looked to him a heaven-sent chance to win the championship. Ray Reardon and John Spencer, who had usually been the players to beat him in the past, were out of the way. There was only me, an unknown, to play in the semis, and either Dennis Taylor, whom he had always beaten, or John Virgo, who had no record to speak of at the time, in the final.

If Alex can fascinate you with his speed, Eddie can mesmerise you – not just with his slowness, but with the identical clockwork way he prepares for each shot. If he plays a million shots, Eddie will methodically follow exactly the same routine. If the rest of him was blacked out, I could always tell it was Eddie by the slow, deliberate way he places his bridge hand on the table. In no way is this a criticism of him, as everybody has his natural tempo. When there is little pressure, I can play very fast, addressing the cue-ball only two or three times before I strike. In matches, I tend to take more time and more care, without taking so much of either that I lose my rhythm.

Eddie is also slow to choose his shot. Many, many times it was obvious to me what he was going to do before he had decided himself, though there are occasions when he, like many players, pretends to consider one shot while he is actually using the time to gather his efforts to attempt another. For a player of his standard, he is very conservative in his choice of shot, particularly in his avoidance of the use of side. Using side makes the pot more difficult but is frequently necessary in order to keep prime position and thus keep the break flowing.

Eddie is so unwilling to increase the possibility of missing a pot that he tends to keep drifting more and more out of position until he has to settle for a safety shot. Although he is a very good potter, he does not risk as many long pots as he might, so, again, with the safety shots he plays and draws his opponent into playing, the balls tend to drift under cushions and get generally tied up. In this way, frames often develop into battles of attrition.

The match started well for me. Eddie, behind that mask of a face which never gives anything away, showed his anxiety by missing a blue which would have given him the first frame, and I made 101 in the second to lead 2-0. I led 4-3 at the first interval, which was overnight, and lost the first frame next day when Eddie was clearly determined, as he usually was, to wear me down with a slow tempo, taking no risks, and with long bouts of safety. Fortunately, I was able to match him at this type of game and whenever the break-making opportunity turned up I was usually able to take it. The seven frames took five hours but I won the last six to lead 10-4.

Six frames in front sounds a lot, even in a 37-frame match, but I was certain, knowing Eddie, that this sort of situation would bring the best out of him in the evening session. His tactics were the same, if anything even more negative than they had been, but instead of making the occasional mistake – he had missed a couple of blacks from the spot in the afternoon – he made hardly any as he slowly picked away at my lead.

Even frames which Eddie should win quite quickly and comfortably tend to be long drawn-out. A case in point was the frame when I was leading 10-5. Eddie was on the black with one red loose and five more bunched on the top cushion. The black was at a perfect angle to take the cue-ball into the bunch. The reds were set at such an angle to each other that at least one was bound to finish in the vicinity of a pocket. In fact, I would have expected them all to finish in open pottable positions. To my surprise, Eddie chose to roll the black in (as shown in diagram 9) and take the loose red and a pink. This left me needing a snooker. You could say that he was making sure of winning the frame rather than going for a break but I wouldn't look at it like that. I would much have preferred to open the reds and win the frame in a clear-cut fashion with one break, which would also increase my confidence, than get bogged down in an end-of-frame struggle with my opponent playing for snookers.

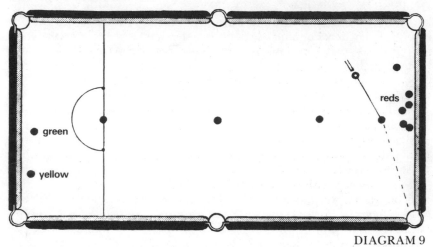

DIAGRAM 9

In fact, despite being 42 behind with only one red remaining, I could have won this frame. As diagram 10 shows, it was easy to push the red on to the baulk cushion and take the cue-ball behind yellow and green, but unfortunately the cue-ball just touched the brown. This meant that Eddie could play off the side cushion with strong right-hand side and

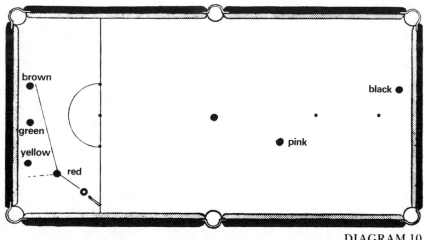

DIAGRAM 10

escape from the snooker easily. If I had got the cue-ball behind the brown, as I had intended, he would have had to shoot up the table, a much more difficult escape.

A couple of shots later, there was another position (diagram 11) from which I could have stolen the game. My idea was to play with left-hand side to bring the cue-ball back behind the brown, while sending the last red up to the yellow, nearly touching it if possible. This could have been not only quite a difficult escape for Eddie but, with the red up against the yellow, a chance for a free ball for me, thus giving me the chance to clear up to win instead of having to play for another snooker. As the diagram shows, I didn't make the snooker difficult enough. I didn't get another chance, so Eddie won the frame. In my opinion, though, he could have lost it through being too negative about going into the bunch earlier.

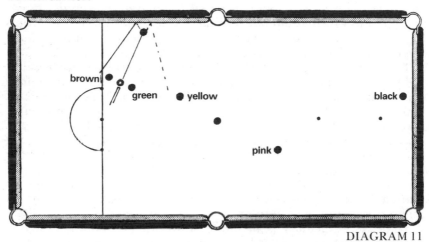

DIAGRAM 11

Eddie's highest break in the session was only 46 but that was the last thing he was interested in. With every frame he won, he started to feel better; for every frame I lost I felt worse. I didn't feel capable of summoning the will and the ability together to change the pattern of the frames. If it's a fast-moving game you are absorbed in the action and don't notice yourself getting tired but this was so long drawn-out that I could feel my concentration disintegrating. Towards the end of the evening, I could feel my eyes getting so tired under the bright television lights that I was not even seeing the balls clearly at a distance.

Having lost the first six frames of the session as Eddie levelled at 10-10, I was resigned to losing the last as well. But I was still stubborn enough to keep trying, and somehow or other I managed to struggle in a good pink to win the frame and lead 11-10 overnight. Once in front was nothing like as good as six in front, but it was psychologically important still to be one-up after such a disastrous session.

Next afternoon it was more of the same – two hours, twelve minutes for the first four frames – except that I was fresh again and felt capable of taking any chances which came my way. Having won two of these four frames to lead 13-12 at the mid-session interval, I won the next frame on the black with a 52 clearance which meant that Eddie, having been within one ball of levelling the match, was now two frames behind. I won the next as well while he was still down, to lead 15-12.

In the last frame, which again took the total playing time for the session over the five-hour mark, I needed two snookers on the colours and got them! Eventually, I had an awkward black with the half-butt which would have put me four up with nine to play going into the final session. If I had potted it, I would have been an odds-on favourite. Eddie would have been kicking himself during the interval for letting such a crucial frame slip away whereas I would have been delighted with a bonus which would have left me needing only three frames out of nine. When I missed the black, though, it meant that my interval lead was only 15-13 and also renewed Eddie's hopes.

Two in front going into the final session was better than two behind, but Eddie won the first two frames of the evening. In the next, almost for the first time in the championship, I didn't clear up when I had a straightforward chance with all the colours open. Anxious to make sure I screwed back far enough from the green, I screwed back too far, leaving the cue-ball under the cushion and failing to pot the brown.

Leading 16-15 was the first time Eddie had been in front. It had been a big psychological effort for him – it had taken him two days to get there from six behind – and he perhaps couldn't apply himself quite so hard in the next frame which I won comfortably to make it 16-16 at the mid-session interval.

The crisis of the match came in the thirty-fourth frame. Eddie led 17-16 and by 44 points to 28. There were two reds left (see diagram 12), one of them very near the middle pocket. The cue-ball was almost on the opposite side cushion but Eddie is so good from this sort of position – or any awkward position – that I expected him to have no trouble in potting that red, plus one of the colours that was easily available, and then enough balls to leave me needing snookers. Had he done so, he would have led 18-16 and I would have had to win the last three frames. I wouldn't have given up but I don't think I could have done it.

When Eddie missed the red (shot 1) it left me a long, almost straight pot (shot 2). I went for it, stunning the cue-ball off the side cushion. The red hit the jaw and as it came back down the table kissed the cue-ball, flicking it behind the pink and leaving a snooker – a bit of luck for me.

Eddie attempted his escape off the side cushion (diagram 13, shot 1) but went between the two reds, leaving me almost on the baulk cushion

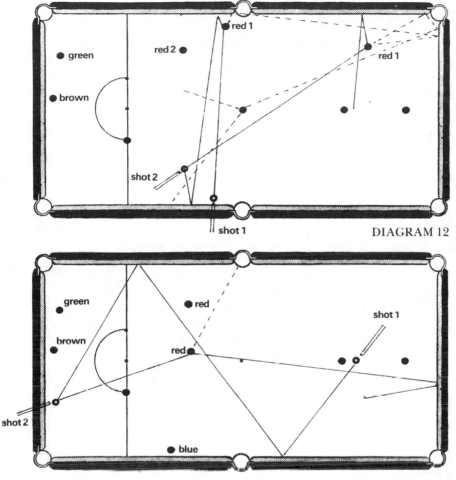

DIAGRAM 12

DIAGRAM 13

with a possible red into the middle. This wasn't easy, particularly as it was in my mind that the cue-ball looked as if it would kiss the pink. The cue-ball just shaved past it, though (shot 2), to leave me a cut black (diagram 14, shot 1 – see next page) which I had to play with a touch of check (left-hand) side to avoid kissing the pink as I attempted to get position on the last red.

These little touch shots can easily go wrong if tension creeps into your arm, but if anything, I played this one too well as the cue-ball finished only a couple of inches away from the last red to give me almost a straight pot into the middle pocket. The trouble was that cue-ball and red were so close together (diagram 14, shot 2) that I couldn't stroke through for fear of a push. I had to jab it and the red caught the bump of the pocket.

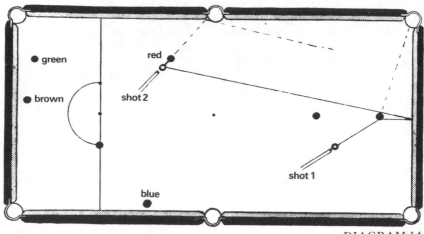

DIAGRAM 14

The score was now 44-40 to Eddie and with the last red finishing in a very pottable position, he had another chance to clinch the game (diagram 15). He must have been feeling the pressure very badly because the pot didn't go all that near the pocket. Luck was on his side this time as he fluked a snooker behind the pink.

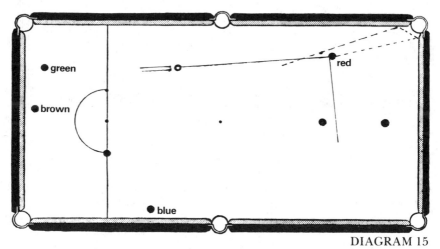

DIAGRAM 15

The obvious escape was off the side cushion (diagram 16, shot 1) and it did cross my mind that the angle at which the cue-ball would rebound gave me a chance of potting the red in the opposite middle pocket. It's the sort of shot you might set up twenty times and not get once, but when I'm in a certain frame of mind I start to think that I can get anything. Though it was more hope than anything else, I just had the feeling the red might go in and so it did, sweet as a nut.

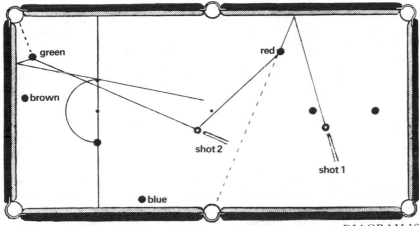

DIAGRAM 16

Playing with the rest, I then took the green (diagram 16, shot 2) just stroking gently through the cue-ball, a plain ball shot, to leave position on the yellow. This is not the sort of shot I particularly like with the rest, as I would much rather be playing with stun, punching through the ball. Although the table was very fast, it was perhaps a bit of anxiety creeping in which made me overhit slightly so that I had another rest shot on the yellow (diagram 17, shot 1), again a gentle push through to bring the cue-ball on and off the baulk cushion.

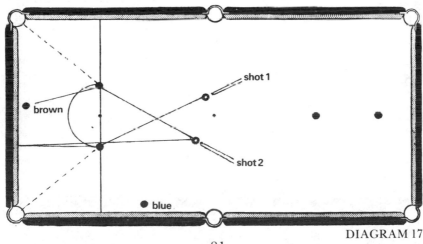

DIAGRAM 17

I thought the cue-ball had landed at the perfect angle to pot the green and knock the brown out (diagram 17, shot 2) but I didn't catch it quite right. The cue-ball double-kissed the brown and finished right on top of it in one of those awful positions where you can't make up your mind what to do for the best.

I considered several possibilities. First, I thought I might take the long rest and chip the right of the brown very thinly, taking the cue-ball well down the table and hardly moving the brown. I ruled this out partly because there was a danger of knocking the brown too near the baulk pocket but mostly because I could not get the long tackle out of the way quickly enough to avoid a foul. Second, I thought of clipping the other side of the brown very thin but there was a danger of kissing the blue. Third, I thought I might push the brown past the middle pocket and leave it between the middle and top pockets – but the snag here was that on the very fast cloth I might well leave the brown quite easily pottable in the top pocket.

Finally (diagram 18, shot 1) I decided to try to send the brown between the blue and the middle pocket and towards the top part of the table, putting as much distance as possible between cue-ball and brown.

After all this, which took several minutes, I misjudged the angle – easy enough to do as cue-ball and brown were very close and brown was very close to the cushion. The brown shot into the middle pocket to leave me nine in front.

I therefore needed only one of the last three balls to leave Eddie needing a snooker. The blue was on the side cushion at just the angle to take the cue-ball up towards the black for a safety shot. It was also just right for the corner pocket double (diagram 18, shot 2). I fancied getting it, though I took the cue-ball down the table in case I missed.

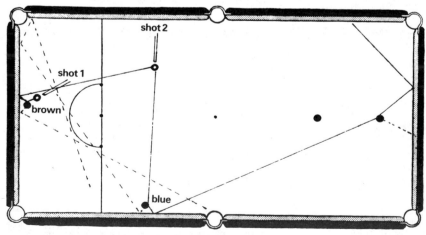

DIAGRAM 18

82

# A FORTNIGHT AT THE CRUCIBLE

The blue didn't go in. The cue-ball caught the black and knocked it under the top cushion. The cue-ball itself finished on the side cushion.

From this, Eddie played a safety shot (diagram 19) attempting, I think, to clip the blue very thin and leave it under the baulk cushion. He actually caught the blue much thicker and doubled it off the side baulk and side cushions to leave me a pottable long blue.

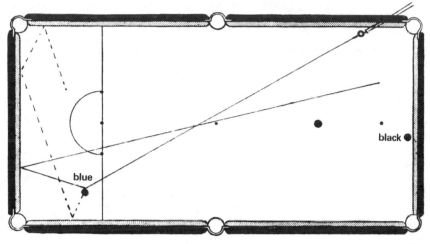

DIAGRAM 19

I was most disappointed not to pot the blue (diagram 20) but, having missed, I was very pleased to see it run safe.

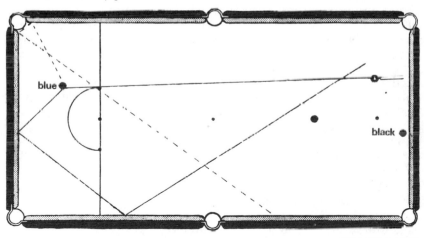

DIAGRAM 20

Eddie then tried to screw off the blue (diagram 21) with a little left-hand side and a thick contact to send the blue off the opposite side cushion and leave it near the middle of the baulk cushion. He also attempted to play a cannon on the black, which, with a full contact, would have stopped the cue-ball, possibly snookering me behind the pink. It would also have knocked the black into a more easily pottable position. But he caught the blue too thin, missed the cannon on the black, and left me a pot which was awkward but nevertheless one that I felt I had to go for.

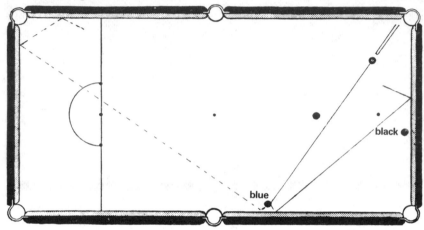

DIAGRAM 21

The pot was almost straight (diagram 22) but against the nap and into a partly-closed pocket. I was thinking so positively by this time that I saw it was a chance to win the frame. I didn't even consider the safety shot. Looking back in cold blood, I can hardly believe I had the nerve to play the shot quite so slowly. Even on the truest of tables you can expect some deviation playing against the nap, but I felt quite confident.

I didn't get the pot, though, and I couldn't have grumbled if I had left the blue in the jaws but, as I've often noticed, if you're feeling good, those vital little rubs of the green tend to go your way. It was here, in fact, that I had my most important piece of luck. As the cue-ball was following through and the blue was coming back off the jaws, they kissed in such a way that Eddie could not pot the blue.

Eddie's safety shot surprised me. I thought he would play very thin off the blue and bring the cue-ball off the opposite side cushion, making the cannon with the black and possibly snookering me behind the pink. Instead (diagram 23), he played slightly thicker on the blue and brought the cue-ball down direct to the top cushion; quite a dangerous shot, I thought, as he could have gone in-off.

This put me in trouble, not as much as I could have been in but quite

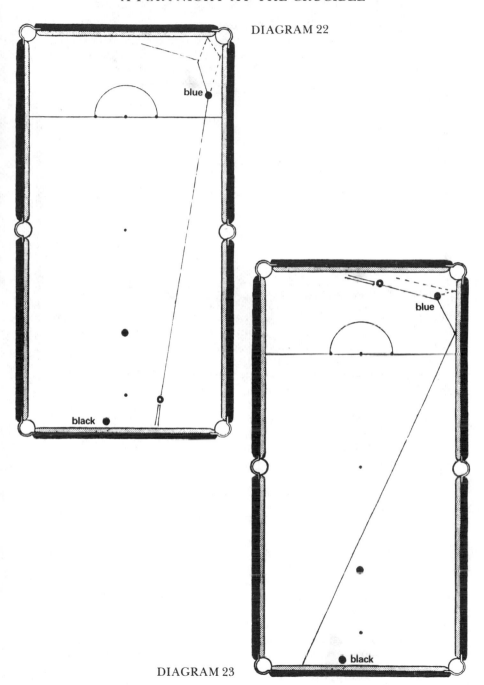

DIAGRAM 22

DIAGRAM 23

85

enough. It was an awkward safety shot for me, the length of the table against the nap. Apart from trying to put some distance between the cue-ball and blue there wasn't much I could do. I doubled the blue up the table (diagram 24) but it finished in the open with the cue-ball just

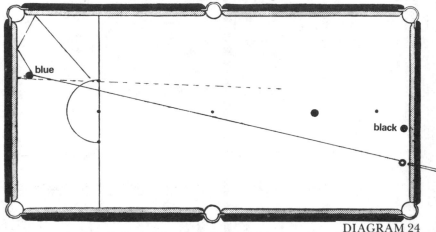

DIAGRAM 24

about on the baulk line. That left Eddie with the sort of pot (diagram 25) which he would get more times than he'd miss, but with the pressure really on he did miss it by quite a margin.

Now, I had a long blue into the yellow pocket (diagram 26). I knocked it in to go 14 in front with only pink and black left. I should then have drifted the pink over the green pocket. Even if I had not potted it, the chances of Eddie cannoning the black out would have been remote. Relaxing my concentration though, I attempted the pink in the middle. I missed, and it did, in fact, give Eddie a chance to cannon the black out. Fortunately, though, he didn't get a snooker and I potted the pink for 17-17. After leading 44-28, Eddie had not potted another ball.

Losing the frame must have been a dreadful blow to Eddie, for had he won it, he would have been two up with three to play. Although I would have tried my hardest I don't think I would have won from that position. With the scores level at 17-17, the odds were now in my favour because Eddie had had the initiative and not taken full advantage of it.

He made two bad mistakes in the next frame – missing a black through overstretching and then missing a straight red with the rest – which let me in for a 69 break and put one up with two to play.

I didn't make a very good start to the thirty-sixth frame. Eddie had left the cue-ball just short of the baulk-line and with the brown just interfering a fraction with my bridge, I fouled it with my sleeve. I didn't feel myself do this, but referee John Williams was in the best position to see and immediately awarded a foul.

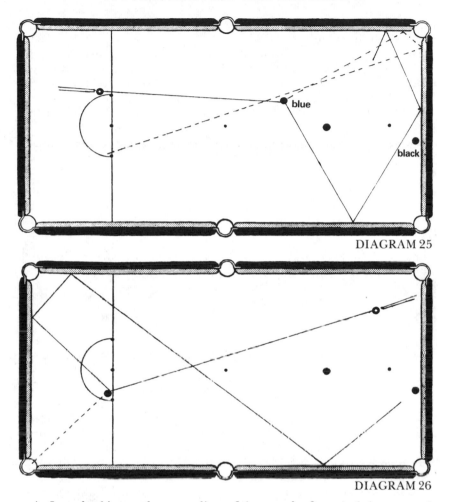

DIAGRAM 25

DIAGRAM 26

As I was looking at the recording of the match afterwards it occurred to me how tired John must have been by then. When you are playing you can at least sit down while your opponent is at the table, but the referee has to stand, hour after hour, ramrod straight, not moving a muscle when a player is on the shot, knowing that one mistake will be remembered and everything else forgotten. It is an unenviable job. John's feet were bleeding at the end of the day.

Having given four away, Eddie was left with the shot I would have had. He had to raise his bridge slightly as he couldn't get his hand on the table in the normal way, but he is usually very good in situations like this and potted the red without any trouble. He scored 16 to lead 20-0, and a few shots later got in again with what looked like developing into the winning break. That would have left the match depending on the thirty-seventh frame.

He scored 23 and left himself on two possible reds near the side cushion (diagram 27, shot 1). I felt that the correct shot was to take the outer red, using a touch of right-hand side for position on the blue. If he had played this well, I am sure Eddie would have taken advantage of the numerous open reds which remained to put the frame out of my reach.

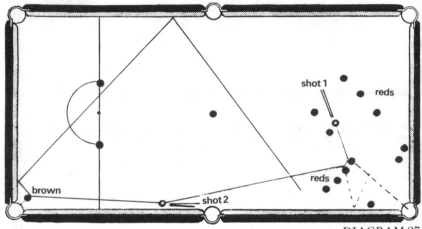

DIAGRAM 27

However, in this position, there is less risk of missing a half-ball pot than one which is quarter-ball. The thicker the contact, the more pocket is in vision as you sight the pot. Eddie decided to pot the inner red even though the cue-ball was certain to cannon the red next to it and leave the cue-ball's ultimate position partly open to chance.

It must have been in Eddie's mind that the brown was within a few inches of the yellow pocket in case position was lost on the blue. In fact, he took the brown (diagram 27, shot 2) but, as can always happen when the cue-ball has to travel several feet (off two cushions in this case), the cue-ball finished in one of those positions where the next shot is missable.

This time Eddie was left a red with the half-butt (diagram 28). It wasn't difficult, but it was more difficult than he would have liked. The red hit the top jaw.

I was down 0-48, and having been sitting out for most of the frame I did not feel my best as I came to the table. My opening stroke (diagram 29, shot 1) was the type of touch shot I would have preferred to play a little later in the break once my arm was swinging freely again. If I had played the pot plain ball the cue-ball would have flicked the inside of the red next to it, and probably not left me very good position on the

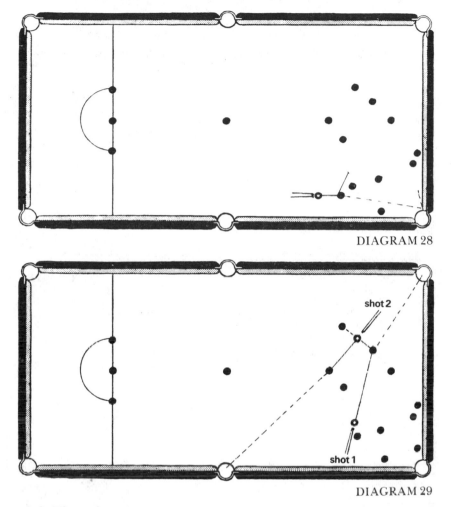

DIAGRAM 28

DIAGRAM 29

pink. The red on the top cushion was blocking the black, so my shot had
to be a slight stun to make sure that I cannoned on to the second red full
ball to leave me on the pink.

Very unusually for me, I got up from my shot. It was good that I had
the self-discipline to do that because if I had played the shot first time,
not feeling quite right, I might have missed it. When I got down the
second time I felt much surer, and the shot came off perfectly to leave
nearly a straight pink into the middle.

Screwing back a couple of inches from the pink (diagram 29, shot 2),
left me an easy red in the corner (diagram 30, shot 1 – see next page),
just bouncing off the cushion to leave an almost straight black. When I

stunned in the black (diagram 30, shot 2) to leave myself on the red near the opposite top pocket, I felt strongly that a clearance was on.

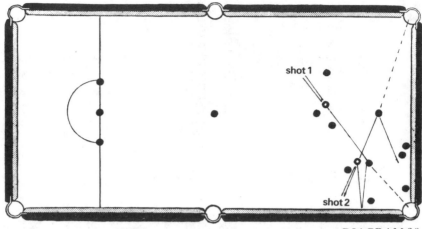

DIAGRAM 30

I ran the red along the cushion (diagram 31) to leave an angle on the black and then screwed down the table (diagram 32) to leave the red just above the pink spot.

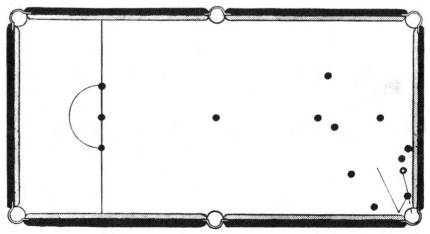

DIAGRAM 31

That left me a rest shot on the next red (diagram 33) from which I decided to punch the cue-ball round off two cushions rather than drift it in slowly to leave the black. Almost straight on the pink, it was a simple stun (diagram 34, shot 1) to leave the next red and from that (diagram 34, shot 2) leave the cue-ball almost straight on the black so

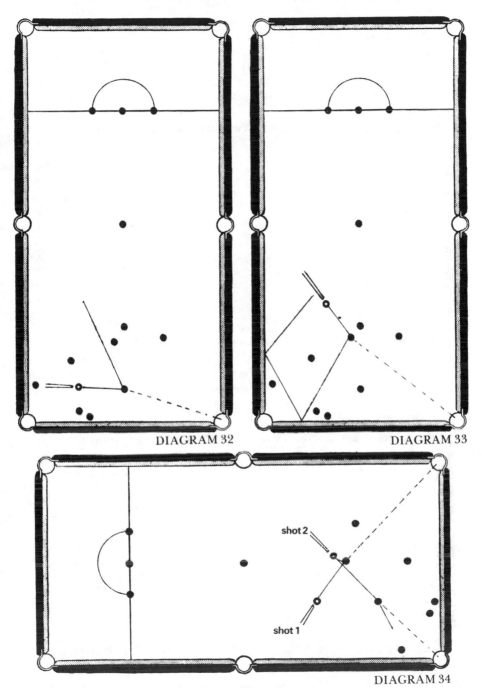

DIAGRAM 32

DIAGRAM 33

shot 2

shot 1

DIAGRAM 34

that I could run through it (diagram 35, shot 1) and leave the outer red, which was lying near the top cushion.

I didn't push through quite far enough on the black, so there was more distance between cue-ball and red than I had intended. The red was also a much more difficult shot than it looked on television as I could only just see enough of the red to pot it. Camera angles seem to distort this type of shot.

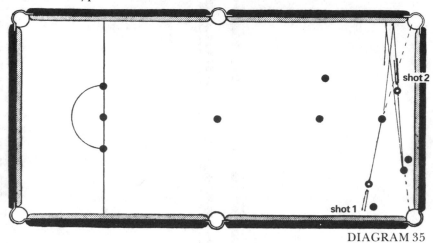

DIAGRAM 35

Potting the red (diagram 35, shot 2) and screwing back off the side cushion left me a slight cut back on the black which I dropped in (diagram 36, shot 1) at just the weight to leave myself on the open red near the pink spot.

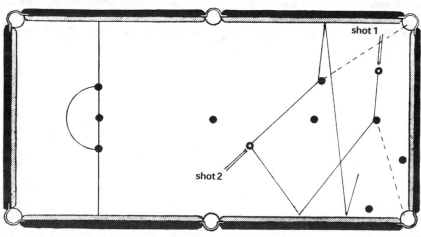

DIAGRAM 36

The red was a natural threequarter-ball run through shot (diagram 36, shot 2) with the cue-ball bouncing off two cushions to leave an almost straight black. A screw back (diagram 37, shot 1) and I had position on the red on the side cushion, not a nice shot as I had to use the half-butt but I felt I would get it (diagram 37, shot 2).

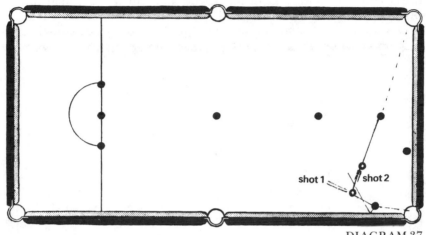

DIAGRAM 37

Again, almost a straight black (diagram 38, shot 1) to stun on to the top cushion for the last red. I stroked this along the top cushion (diagram 38, shot 2) without any side as I wanted to be sure to leave myself the proper angle to pot the black and go down for the colours (diagram 39, shot 1 – see next page).

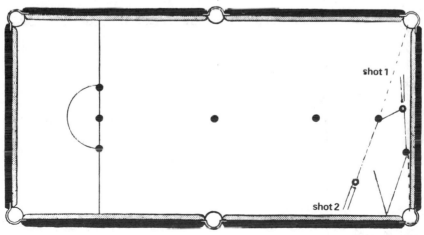

DIAGRAM 38

Potting the black brought my break to 70 but I was still only 22 in front. The yellow, stunning off the side cushion (diagram 39, shot 2), made my lead 24 so I only needed the green to leave Eddie needing a snooker. Once I had potted this (diagram 39, shot 3) to go 27 in front I checked the scoreboard, but I had put so much mental effort into my break that my mind went blank. I wouldn't usually have had much problem subtracting 48 (Eddie's score) from 75 (mine) but I had to stop, wipe my brow, and start again before I could do it this time!

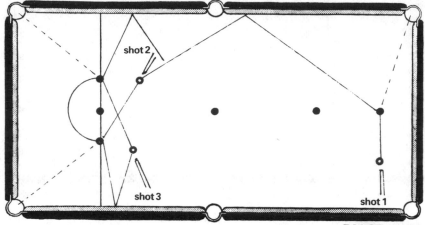

DIAGRAM 39

Once the difference had sunk in, I had a vision of miscueing on the brown attempting a deep screw for the blue, and perhaps throwing the frame away. I doubt that I would have done so but, just to be on the safe side, I stunned the brown in (diagram 40, shot 1), not playing position

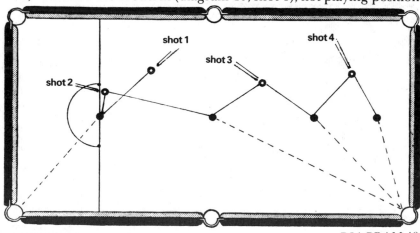

DIAGRAM 40

at all for the blue, to lead by 31 with only 18 points on the table.

I knew I had won. Without a care in the world, I potted the blue (diagram 40, shot 2) in the top pocket. The crowd was on its feet cheering as I potted pink (diagram 40, shot 3) and black (diagram 40, shot 4) for the 97 clearance. I had taken the last nine reds, seven blacks, two pinks and the colours to win the frame 97-48 and the match by 19-17.

---

1979 World Championship
*Semi-finals*
Griffiths beat Eddie Charlton 19-17
I   66-55;     101(101)-38;     20-102(30,33);     70(50)-59;
22-100(54,30); 66-23; 20-69 (Griffiths 4-3)
II   36-67;   76(69)-20;   93(37)-37;   78-22;   83(32,35)-48;
60(31)-35; 114(64)-6 (Griffiths 10-4)
III   25-92(37); 30-72(31); 20-82(38); 11-96(40); 9-66(46);
29-81(36); 66(38)-51(33) (Griffiths 11-10)
IV   78(38)-35;   32-75;   16-81;   76(68)-19;   68(52)-64;
108(35,50)-5; 64-72(36) (Griffiths 15-13)
V   44-76(31); 36(36)-87(44); 45-66; 65(35)-4; 45(41)-79(33);
64-44; 95(69)-9; 97(97)-48

---

I wouldn't attempt to analyse the emotion of a moment like that. So many things are mixed together. There is the relief, the sense of achievement, the raw satisfaction of receiving an unbelievable ovation – and then you become conscious of what the match has meant to other people. Peter came out of the crowd to swing me round and round; my father was crying. I was still in a daze when David Vine stuck a microphone under my nose and started asking me questions. I talked about how tough an opponent Eddie had been, how I had had him all but dead two or three times and how he had kept coming back.

Never before or since have I managed to concentrate so intensely for such a long period, particularly against an opponent whose slow tempo of play puts your concentration under all the more pressure. The last session had taken five hours, twenty-five minutes, which I was told was only ten minutes shorter than the longest-ever professional session. I had lost all track of time but it was 1.40am. There was a lull in David's questions and I suddenly blurted out: 'I'm in the final, now, you know.' I had been so wrapped up in the match that it was only just hitting home that there was a final still to play.

I was in the wrong frame of mind to play Dennis Taylor, who had beaten John Virgo in the other semi-final. He's a good player but he has never been a big name like Higgins or Charlton. I knew he was quite capable of beating me but in some strange way the final was an anti-climax. I seemed to jog along more or less automatically for two days and only really felt that I was playing for the title when we started the last day's play. All along, I thought that if we could go in to the last day more or less level, I would have a very good chance on the run-in.

Winning quite a few amateur finals gave me the confidence to win this time. If you have won a few things you tend to think like a winner when it comes to a vital final. Dennis, who had turned professional

Dennis Taylor, the final hurdle . . .

without much of an amateur record, had not had this background. He had reached the world semi-final both in 1975 and 1977 but he had never won a major tournament. This could well have had something to do with the way his arm seemed to tighten up on the last day whereas the adrenalin which came with the knowledge that *this was it* helped me play better.

Although the cameras had been present throughout the championship fortnight, when the final started I was very conscious that the transmission was live. Although the coverage is done exactly the same whether the play is shown live or recorded, it made an unexpected psychological difference to me. The first frame also turned into a bit of a farce. I started with a good long red, followed by the black to prise another red loose, and then miscued. In fact, I miscued three times in four shots. A small shiny spot might have developed on the tip of my cue but basically it was because I wasn't cueing well. Somehow, I won the frame on the pink and led 3-1 at the mid-session interval.

I stormed into my dressing-room, livid with myself for the way I had played. I wasn't even relieved that Dennis had missed his chance to take advantage of the way I was struggling. I just wanted to play better. Next frame, I made a break of 120 which ended with the brown on the lip of the pocket. The last four colours would have enabled me to equal the championship record break of 142 set by Rex Williams in 1965 and equalled by Bill Werbeniuk in the 1979 championship.

When I led 5-1 and started the last frame of the first session with a 65 break, it looked like 6-1 at the interval until Dennis came to life with a 71 clearance to win on the black.

This was an important frame for him as 2-5 was a lot better than 1-6. With a five-frame lead, you only have to get two or three more in front and it's nearly impossible to be caught. A gap of three, in a long match, is hardly here or there. Anyway, that last frame of the opening session gave Dennis a lot of encouragement and he played much better in the evening. Conversely, I started to labour a bit and for the last three frames of the session my eyes were so tired that I could hardly focus on the balls. He caught me up at 7-7 before I somehow won the last frame of the day to lead 8-7 overnight.

The second day of the final was probably my worst day of the whole championship. I felt, all day, that I was playing against the grain. I was there to be taken and Dennis twice got two frames in front at 11-9 and 14-12. Fortunately, he seemed to lose a bit of confidence in himself when he was in a position to extend his lead. If he had, it might have left me with too much to do on the last day.

I had started the match expecting a good, open type of match but Dennis surprised me time and again by stopping the flow of the game either by playing defensively when attacking shots were there, or making sure of a pot at the expense of his position, or by not opening the balls out when it must have been obvious that I was struggling. I think that, at this level, you have to make up your mind to go out and win rather than wait for your opponent to lose.

The 24th frame with Dennis leading 12-11 (see diagram 41) was a case in point. I had made a 51 break to go 21 in front but Dennis could win with all the colours. He had two chances. First, he had a chance to pot the yellow in a top pocket, holding position for the green with all the other colours open. He refused this in favour of sending the yellow behind the black and bringing the cue-ball behind the green. The cue-ball didn't run quite far enough for the snooker but I cued very badly and hit the black by mistake anyway. Fortunately it didn't leave Dennis a clear-cut chance to win the frame.

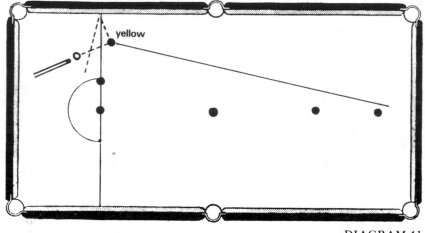

DIAGRAM 41

A little later (diagram 42), Dennis had a chance at a long yellow. Without doubt, I would have gone for it as I firmly believe you are more likely to get a favourable run of the balls if you play a positive type of game. Even if he had not potted the yellow, it might have gone safe. Instead, he doubled the yellow round and failed to snooker me. I took a long yellow, then green, brown and blue for the frame and 12-12.

In the very long frames, of which this was one, Dennis seemed to go more and more defensive near the end whereas I think that at the colours stage you have to attempt anything reasonable. In effect, one good shot at this stage and you have won the frame.

The first frame of the last day was psychologically very important as the opening frame of a session can often set the tone for what is to follow. Dennis was first in with 41 and had another chance to make sure of the frame before he came to the colours leading by 20. I won the frame for two reasons. First, I potted a long yellow (diagram 43), which

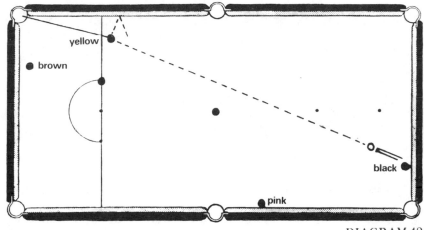

DIAGRAM 42

I don't think Dennis would have attempted if he had had the chance; and second, when I attempted the pink with the rest along the side cushion into a baulk pocket it jawed but went safe, a bit of luck certainly but I felt I deserved it because of the positive shot I had played.

Dennis seemed to let my piece of luck affect him. He looked a bit irritated that the balls had run against him and perhaps started to feel that the gods were not going to be on his side. He misjudged the safety shot and I took pink and black for game. That made it 16-15 and I was never behind again.

Another shot which sticks in my memory came when I was leading 17-16 and by 36 points to 24. There were two reds left (see diagram 44)

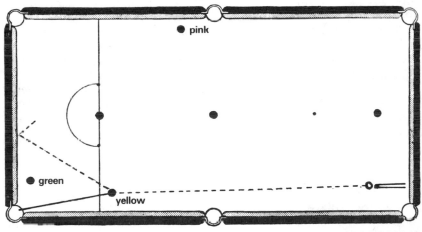

DIAGRAM 43

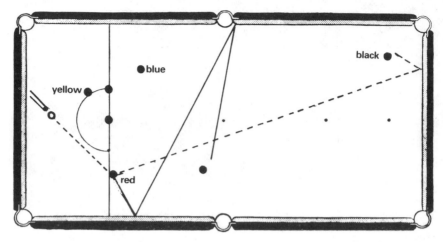

DIAGRAM 44

and I attempted the cross double in such a way that I was taking the cue-ball behind the black for a snooker, or possibly to pot the black if the red went in. As it happened, the red struck the lip of the middle pocket and bounced straight back. Dennis was snookered, leaving me the chance I needed to clinch the frame. It had lasted fifty minutes and was very scrappy in parts, but it put me two in front at 18-16 and gave me the confidence to play well.

I had seven breaks between 35 and 71 in the remaining four frames of the session, and led 22-16 at the interval.

I felt so good that at 21-16 and 47 points to 43 I had the confidence to attempt quite a difficult red down the side cushion (see diagram 45) instead of taking the much easier red first. I did this because I felt I might not get any better position on the awkward red. Had I been five frames behind instead of five in front, it might not have looked so easy. When the red went in, it seemed quite straightforward to clear up.

Going into the final session six in front with nine to play was a marvellous feeling. It was good for me that I had had the experience of losing 9-8 to Rex Williams in the Coral UK Championship earlier in the season because this stopped me feeling that the rest was a formality. I only had to win two frames, but I knew that if Dennis won the first two or three and got a charge going it could still be tough. I knew it was important not to give him the slightest encouragement.

Even when I won the first frame 117-0 to go seven up with eight to play, I didn't relax. At the start of the next frame I scored nine and in preference to playing to the gallery with a risky, exhibition-type shot, I rolled up dead behind the green. I made 56 from my next opening and I was champion.

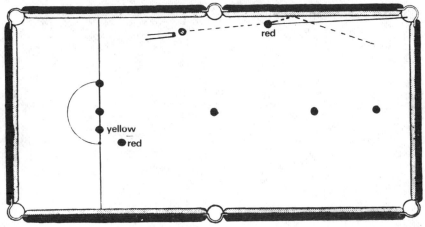

DIAGRAM 45

1979 World Championship
*Final*
Griffiths beat Dennis Taylor 24-16
I   67-51;   63-54(39);   37 66;   75(56)-49(40);   120(120)-9;
106(41)-24; 65(65)-71(71) (Griffiths 5-2)
II   1-91(31);   45-64;   84(33,34)-38;   22-66(57);   60(31)-10;
3-97(69); 57(30)-66; 89(43)-40(36) (Griffiths 8-7)
III   42-66(40); 32-83(70);   69(43)-49; 22-86(35);   16-92(92);
94(38,34)-31; 85(36,45)-35 (11-11)
IV   12-84;   76(51)-41;   4-90(84);   36-66(47);   94(49)-15;
59(37)-22; 54-67; 73(35)-27 (15-15)
V   60-53(41);   127(64,44)-2;   51(32)-62(39);   67(31)-24;
115(71)-5; 104(48,48)-1; 77(35,42)-16; 84(38,37)-43 (Griffiths
22-16)
VI   117(37,31,49)-0; 92(56)-16

'From the Llanelli League to this', said my father at the reception afterwards. I was very happy, of course, though not quite so elated as I would have been if it had been a close finish. Going into the last session six in front had given me the kind of advance warning which means that winning does not come as such a shock to the system. The implications of the victory had not really sunk in, though I did realise that I was more or less made financially and that my new status as champion would mean big changes in my life. For the moment, though, all I wanted to do was get home.

101

# ─── 7 ───
# Aftermath

My first day as champion I spent in a ten-hour meeting of the World Professional Billiards and Snooker Association in the St George Hotel, Sheffield, where several of the players had stayed for the championship. As professional snooker is run entirely by the players, meetings can't be avoided. To some extent I enjoy them but this one went on so long and was so confusing that even when it was over I was not sure what had been agreed.

The meeting split the professional game into two camps, mainly because a change in the world championship conditions was forced through: this meant that instead of the top eight in the WPBSA ranking list, only the champion and runner-up from the preceding year would be exempted from the qualifying competition and therefore be sure of playing at Sheffield on television. The change of rule didn't directly affect me – or Dennis Taylor – for one year, but some of snooker's biggest names, like Ray Reardon, Alex Higgins, John Spencer and Eddie Charlton, all had to qualify. Understandably, they were not very pleased.

The problem was that the eight professionals who, under the old system, were sure of playing at Sheffield were heavily outnumbered by those who had to qualify. Those who belonged to this bigger group reckoned that with fourteen places available from the qualifying competition instead of eight, their chances of winning through to Sheffield would naturally be all the greater.

There had been rumblings for a long time that WPBSA decisions were being influenced too much by players who were not very successful. Ray Reardon felt particularly strongly about this and played a big part in founding Professional Snooker Association Ltd, known in the game as PSA. All the leading players, Dennis and myself included, joined because the new organisation seemed to offer some kind of solidarity and strength in numbers in dealing with promoters, sponsors and television companies. As it stood, we felt that the WPBSA was worse than useless in this respect.

It is obvious from the choice of name that PSA Ltd was also set up so that it could, if necessary, become an alternative governing body for professional snooker. Fortunately, this split did not happen. After months of wrangling, the game's affairs were sorted out – not perhaps to everybody's satisfaction, but in a way that everybody could accept.

The WPBSA's constitution was changed so that the top ten in the ranking list automatically constituted the committee. In effect, the top players now made the important decisions. The top eight in the ranking list, as in previous years, were exempted until the last sixteen, but in order to give more players a chance of playing on television at Sheffield the field was extended to twenty-four. Numbers nine to sixteen in the rankings automatically played in the first round at Sheffield, and the other eight came, as before, from the jungle of the qualifying competition.

Now that things have settled down, the decisions seem very logical and clear-cut but at the time it was chaos. Close friends like Rex Williams and Fred Davis fell out badly when they found themselves on different sides. Hanging over all of us, too, was the threat that in all the wrangling everything might disintegrate so far that television and sponsors might find themselves another sport. My ear was bent first by one side and then the other and the whole business caused me more worry in my first few months as champion than anything else.

When I eventually got away from Sheffield it really began to sink in that I had won. I had spent a fortnight in the glossy surroundings of the Crucible in a very intense, 'sealed off' atmosphere. Travelling from Sheffield, I was also travelling towards everything that I thought of as normal life and it wasn't until I got home that I suddenly realised what my success looked like through the eyes of the people that I knew.

Even a world championship is still, when you get down to the bones of it, a snooker tournament. I had played in hundreds of them, winning and losing, so this was just another that I was doing my best in as a player. I had been conscious of the setting and importance of the championship, but only as additional stimulants to what I had done countless times before.

A big crowd was there to greet me when I arrived home – among them Steve Davis, who was to beat me in the 1980 championship, whom I had booked in for a couple of shows in the area as a return favour for those his manager, Barry Hearn, had done for me. Outside my house there were rows of flags stretched from rooftops to lamp posts and a great big red and white 'welcome home champ' banner. It took something like that to make me realise what my success had meant to other people, and what the atmosphere must have been like in the town. I learnt later that when the snooker hadn't been on the television, half Llanelli had been ringing up the press room at the Crucible, four or five times a frame some of them, to ask the latest score. Quite a few had backed me at my starting price of 66-1.

My house was full of long lost aunties and uncles. I saw my children for the first time in a fortnight. We didn't need to drink to celebrate –

Welcome home!

just all of us being together at such a time was the celebration.

There was one phone call after another. Press, radio and television were in and out of my house for days. The John Rees bakery in town presented me with a huge cake (worth £170) made in the shape of a snooker table with green icing as baize, and brown marzipan wood-work. I left my car on double yellow lines and the traffic warden guarded it.

My first playing engagement after winning the championship was at the village club in Kilgetty. They had booked me when I was nobody and suddenly found they had booked the world champion. The bookings poured in and a contract to play a summer season at Butlins holiday camps, which had been in the air before the championship, was confirmed.

Reconstructing a typical fortnight from my diary, I would leave home on Sunday night to drive to Filey in Yorkshire to play at the Butlins camp there on Monday afternoon. I drove to Skegness to play at another camp on Tuesday morning and then to Birmingham for a pool exhibition for a brewery in one of their pubs. Late at night I drove on to Clacton where I had to play another Butlins show at 2pm on Wednesday. If I had left the journey to the morning it would have taken me twice as long in all the traffic.

From Clacton, I was straight on the road to Bedford for another exhibition at a new snooker centre before driving home in the early hours. Thursday, I had appointments with my dentist and my solicitor, and Friday was an easy day, just up to Barry for a Butlins show in the afternoon. I had Saturday off, but I had been given the key to a new snooker centre which was about to open in Llanelli and took the opportunity for a little quiet practice. As this was before I had been able to have a table installed at home, I had hardly practised since the championship as there was no way that I could go into a club as I used to and just be left alone.

On the Sunday and Monday nights I played exhibitions in the London area. I spent most of Monday with my agents. Tuesday, Wednesday and Thursday afternoons I played Butlins shows at Bognor, Minehead and Pwllheli with an evening show at Chester on the Thursday. I had Friday and Saturday off before getting on the road to Filey again on Sunday night.

## AFTERMATH: AN OUTSIDE VIEW by Clive Everton

Two months later, a hint of crow's-feet around his eyes, Terry parked outside Cheltenham Fire Station after a hot, frustrating afternoon at Barry on the last leg of his weekly Butlins circuit. There are some two hundred spectators in the station's snooker room. The table is right by the double doors to the fireman's pole. One has a vision of alarm bells ringing and men rather than snooker balls disappearing downwards.

'It's the big one for us', says the man who takes us up to the committee room. 'Getting him so soon after winning the championship.'

Peter Francis, now acting as Terry's driver and road manager, sets off for a round of drinks. Terry's father, a huge retired steelworker, massively overflows a chair.

More figures appear. There are sheepish requests for autographs. 'He's shorter than you think from the telly', one man confides. 'Ray Reardon did a 96 and the black wobbled in the pocket when he was here', says another.

Terry grins a trifle wearily, acknowledging the disparity between what is implicitly expected of him and what at that tired moment he feels capable of. With quiet diplomacy he clears the committee room and starts to change into a dress suit, liberally applying cool spray talc to his feet ('You're on your feet so much you need something'), lamenting the lack of a mirror, and talking of some of the bizarre offers which have come his way since he became champion.

'There's this record, see. No, I don't have to sing. I can't sing. They do it in the studio somehow. They say I'll make £20,000 out of it. Or £200,000, I don't know. When I told Annette she said: "You'll make a bloody fool of yourself." I don't want to do it myself but you can't say no just like that, can you?'

# AFTERMATH

He is just in the process of terminating his management contract with the International Snooker Agency, whose directors at that time were two former world champions, Ray Reardon and John Spencer, and the day-to-day organiser of the company's business, Del Simmons.

'When I first turned professional there wasn't really an alternative, but when I won the championship a few other possibilities came up, London companies who know about advertising and television.'

In the changeover period he is grappling with his own affairs, trying to choose between two attractive contracts to endorse cues. He is starting to appreciate that champions tend to be very highly taxed. 'I've never had enough money to worry about it before', he says.

'He's more on pins now than when he played in the championship', says Peter Francis. 'He's not happy. He's as snappy as hell. Day before yesterday, he did Butlins at Clacton in the afternoon and a show at Billericay at night. I told him he should stay over and drive home when he was fresh but no, he wouldn't have it. Quarter to five we got in. Then up at eight-thirty to take the kids to school. He's knocking himself out.'

'The eldest boy's pining for me just now', says Terry. 'He's cuddling into me when I'm home. He never used to do that. When the phone goes, he gets an upset stomach. He's not used to me being away so much, see. During the championship and after there was all the excitement from the television and press. The phone was going all the time and it unsettled him.'

The exhibition starts unexpectedly. Terry whacks the cue-ball off the side and top cushions to scatter the triangle of reds, but the cushions are not of championship quality. The cue-ball hurdles the triangle and ends up on the floor. Within a very few shots it also transpires that the cue-ball is lighter than it should be and is throwing some strange angles. Peter is despatched to the car for another cue-ball, but the snooker remains tough going, the corner pockets so tight that shots along the cushion or from narrow angles look doomed to failure without the aid of a shoe-lift.

At the interval, after four of the evening's eight frames, his highest break is 32. He slips away to phone Annette, as he does every day, and sips a cup of tea. When the second half of the show starts, he looks subtly different, cueing more freely and absorbed in what he is doing. The balls split favourably for a break and it is suddenly inconceivable that he can miss. A break of 108 and he has made everybody's night. 'It's a good cup of tea they make here', he quips.

At 12.20 he stands in the car park. 'I couldn't keep this up you know. I want a few good contracts so I don't have to play every night. I want to spend some time at home and prepare properly for the big tournaments instead of dashing about like this. I'll be all right once I get myself organised.' Then he left, to drive home to Llanelli with his father and Peter.

# 8

# A Champion's Year

By the end of the summer I was so shattered that I approached the first tournament of the new season, the Canadian Open in Toronto in the last week in August, as if I was on holiday. This was justified to some extent as it is played as part of the annual Canadian National Exhibition which has a funfair, sports events, pop concerts, cattle shows, trade stands, and all sorts of attractions on one big site. Next to the snooker was a fashion show with electric organ accompaniment, and a stand advertising the Mounties which had a police siren blaring every five minutes. It was very hot, spectators wandered in and out, and conditions were very difficult. Everyone was very friendly and Toronto itself was a very clean and attractive city to visit – but I did find it difficult to motivate myself. I beat Derek Norris 9-6 and Jim Wych 9-2 but Kirk Stevens had every chance to beat me in the semi-final.

Kirk led 3-0 and at 6-4 missed a straightforward colours clearance which would have made it 7-4. He still led 7-5 and at 8-7 made a mess of another colours clearance which would have given him the match. I scraped through 9-8, under no illusions that Kirk, who had tensed up badly in sight of victory, had thrown the match away through inexperience.

---

1979 Canadian Open
*Semi-finals*
Griffiths beat Kirk Stevens 9-8
7-111(81); 24-64; 20-73(43); 60-50; 81(46)-21; 76(56)-0;
22-64; 84-30; 53-67; 44-72; 61-40; 13-113(95); 54-8;
111(46,65)-0; 2-70; 77(59)-40; 82-4

---

Cliff Thorburn, who had beaten Alex Higgins 9-6 in the other semi-final, is a tough opponent at the best of times. His deliberate, methodical style grinds down the concentration and willpower of his opponents. Once he gets into a groove it is very difficult to shake him. On top of that, he is even better in Canadian conditions than British, so it is impossible to beat him without working very hard.

I didn't work hard enough. The final was two days and 33 frames and in that heat and noise it seemed, at the start, like an eternity. I had decided to attack, to get the frames over quickly one way or the other, but hardly any of my long pots went in. This may not have been entirely my fault, because however many I missed I always fancied getting the next and my cueing felt all right. What was happening, I think, on a thin cloth in hot conditions, was that the cue-ball was not staying on line on the bed of the table as it would have done in British conditions with a thick cloth, a thick slate and a cooler atmosphere.

Cliff kept sweeping up like clockwork from my mistakes, and led 10-3 before I found a bit of form at the end of the day with breaks of 81, 109 and 88 to make it 10-6.

My attitude was much better on the second day, just as it had been for the last day of the world final against Dennis Taylor. I won a couple of frames to make it 10-8, threw the next away with three bad mistakes, but caught up to 12-12 by winning the last two frames before the interval.

I won the first frame of the final session but I hardly did anything in the next three and lost them all. Looking back, this was where the match was lost – though you could also say that Cliff did his best to lose by the way he played the next two frames!

Cliff's weakness as a match player over the years has been clinching winning positions. He tends to play his best when he is level or one or two frames behind, not so well when he is a frame or two in front. If he is a long way ahead and can get rid of the anxiety of letting slip a winning position, he will play better and better.

At 15-15, with three to play, I was very unlucky. Needing the last three balls to win, I potted the blue and kissed the pink off the side cushion as I had intended. Unfortunately, the pink rolled into the opposite middle pocket, so instead of being one up with two to play I was one down.

In the next frame, the last red was on the edge of the baulk pocket with the green right next to it. From this position, I had four consecutive four-point penalties plus, inevitably, four free balls as Cliff strug-

---

1979 Canadian Open
*Final*
Cliff Thorburn beat Griffiths 17-16
I   39-98; 80-37; 64-30; 59-8; 5-114(73); 13-104(63); 67-48; 69-21 (Thorburn 5-3)
II   69-56; 101(81)-0; 80(50)-23; 7-40; 74-38; 40-86(81); 0-109(109); 32-88(88) (Thorburn 10-6)
III   43-70; 21-57; 64-41; 20-67(42); 51-62; 98(94)-36; 17-67; 21-81 (12-12)
IV   57(40)-72; 75(75)-0; 55-19; 72-7; 36-57; 11-67; 77-50; 40-90; 73-49

gled with the almost impossible task of hitting the red. By the time he managed to break up the position he already needed snookers.

In the decider, Cliff was 26 in front when he fluked the last red out of a snooker, which meant that I could only draw with the colours. Trying the green, for the match, Cliff knocked the black in, but I couldn't get a clear-cut chance. Finally, he snookered me on the brown, and in getting out of the snooker I left the brown on.

I had not had a very good run of the balls in the last two or three frames but I couldn't say I had been unlucky to lose. You sometimes see fights where one boxer puts in a grandstand finish but doesn't get the verdict. The crowd jumps up and down, booing and shouting, forgetting that the other man has won most of the earlier rounds by a street. Something similar had happened here. Every frame which Cliff had won so easily on the first day, before the match had even approached a climax, counted the same as the ones I won near the end when it was getting exciting. If I had really applied myself from the start the gods might have favoured me when it was neck and neck at the end. When the luck went against me I knew I hadn't really deserved to have it run in my favour.

I didn't realise until it was too late what a mistake it had been to lose. Ray Reardon had told me how important it was for the champion to consolidate by winning everything in sight to build up, if he could, a mental barrier between himself and the other players. It is always hard to beat top players, but if he can string enough successes together to create an illusion of 'unbeatability', as Ray had done in the mid-seventies, opponents tend to become over-anxious if they ever do get near to beating him. Losing to Cliff in Canada was one chance missed, and losing to John Virgo in the Coral United Kingdom final a couple of months later was to be another.

I left Toronto the night after the final and arrived at Heathrow at breakfast time. I drove Annette home, took an air taxi from Swansea to Leeds and won three one-frame matches – against Willie Thorne, Rex Williams and Dennis Taylor – to win a one-night tournament at the Queens Hotel, sponsored by Acrilan Carpets. I hadn't been to bed for forty-eight hours!

My first major tournament appearance in Britain since becoming champion, though, was in the first ever world team championship, the State Express World Cup, at Haden Hill Leisure Centre, near Birmingham. The Welsh team of Doug Mountjoy, Ray Reardon and myself were favourites, but we were looking sick in our first match when Canada led us 4-0. Ray had lost 3-0 to Kirk Stevens, Doug had lost a frame to Cliff Thorburn, and I was struggling against Bill Werbeniuk until I fluked the pink to make it 4-1 instead of 5-0.

The format was that opposite numbers (i.e. number one v number one, number two v number two, and number three v number three)

The State Express World Cup 1979 – Wales triumphant! With me, Doug Mountjoy (far left) and Ray Reardon.

played three frames against each other, plus one frame each against the other two opposing players. This made the match fifteen frames in all. It was difficult for the players because, instead of settling down to play a session of seven or eight frames, they were constantly stopping and starting. There is also a special tension in playing for a team, particularly a national team, and even more so when we were aware how disappointed Welsh snooker people would be if we didn't win the title.

Ray beat Cliff to make it 2-4 and then Doug won a key frame against Kirk, the last before the interval. This took an hour and ended in a tie. Kirk twice had a clear shot at the re-spot black which would have put Canada 5-2 up at the interval before Doug eventually potted it to keep the margin to 3-4.

We were struggling again at 3-5 when Bill made a frame-winning 58 after Ray had been in first with 41. I beat Kirk but the vital contribution was Doug winning all three frames against Bill, including two black ball finishes.

This put us 7-5 up with me to play last, three frames against Cliff. I felt a lot of pressure, even more when Cliff won the first with a break of 126. The second frame was close but I had a really crucial piece of luck, fluking the yellow out of a snooker, so at 8-6 we had won.

Our other qualifying match, against Australia, who on paper were much weaker, wasn't easy either. Having led 5-1 we lost the next three and it was only 7-5 when I went on last for my three frames against Gary Owen, who was actually born in Tumble, just outside Llanelli.

Gary was a fireman in Birmingham when he won his two World Amateur titles in 1963 and 1966. He lost to John Spencer in the 1969 World Professional final but had more or less drifted out of the competitive game in the mid-seventies after emigrating to Australia. He had come into the Australian team only as a late replacement for Eddie Charlton, but in short matches he could still do enough to be troublesome. He won the first to make it 6-7 but I got in twice in the next frame with 39 and 63 and we were through to the final.

England had beaten the Rest of the World 8-7 and Northern Ireland 8-7 to win the other group. They had three good players (Fred Davis, John Spencer and Graham Miles) but they never really gave the impression of being a team. None of them played well and we won very easily 14-3.

Although the final was an anti-climax, the tournament did prove that there was a future for team snooker at this level. As the game grows there will be more countries involved, which is going to enhance the status of the event and make snooker more international.

There were some weeks before the next major tournament, the Coral United Kingdom Championship at Preston Guildhall, but I was here, there and everywhere with exhibition matches. My whole life seemed to be motorways and snooker tables. One Sunday morning I was driving from Llanelli to Scarborough when I lost my concentration for a second or two on the M62 just outside Leeds. Before I knew what was happening my car was careering from one side of the road to the other.

Alan Armstrong, who was promoting the match in the Stephen Joseph Theatre, was very surprised to hear from me at about 10.30am. My car was a write-off, I was very shaken up, and I was wondering how I was going to get to Scarborough. Alan set out to pick me up but broke down in the wilds and had to hitch a lift even to reach me. Another lift got us to the Crest Hotel, Leeds, but it was now one o'clock. I was due to play at two, Scarborough was two hours away and we had no transport.

At this point, a man asked me for my autograph. He sensed something was wrong and when we told him what the problem was, he immediately packed his wife and son off home by taxi and drove us to Scarborough.

We arrived at the theatre at three o'clock to find all the audience still outside. My opponent, Jimmy White, who that year had won the English Amateur Championship at the age of sixteen, the youngest-ever winner, had not shown up. As he had been playing in Manchester the night before, he only had to catch the train to York and be picked up but something had gone wrong. Incredibly, only one ticket-holder took up Alan's offer of 'money back' as I spent the afternoon playing members of the audience. Alan meanwhile ran Jimmy to earth and got him to the theatre in time for the evening session. I don't know who was in worse shape by the end of the day, Alan or I.

By the time the UK tournament started in November, I was jaded and also having tip problems. I couldn't seem to get one which felt right and, while I was switching from one to another and playing them in, my game was falling apart. Cliff Wilson was my first opponent. If he had really been buzzing he could have been dangerous, but he had problems of his own at the time with his eyes and his cue, and was never really a threat. I won 9-4.

That put me against Higgins in the quarter-finals. I hadn't been playing well but I didn't like the idea of losing to Alex so I was keyed up for a big effort.

A few weeks before, he had hammered me 8-1 in an exhibition at Tenby, which was fair enough; but at Deeside Leisure Centre, when he again beat me 4-2, he had really annoyed me. When I was playing the trick shots at the end of the evening, I missed the basket shot twice. 'Let me do it', shouted Alex. It is inexcusable to belittle another player in this way, but I just let him get on with it. I just thought to myself: 'His day will come.'

It was a very good match. I led 5-2 at the interval; he led 7-5; I won 9-7.

Bill Werbeniuk, who, although he is a Canadian, qualifies for the UK because he is permanently resident here, had beaten John Spencer and Ray Edmonds, both 9-8, to become my next opponent. The first session was a bit scrappy with both of us failing to clinch frame-winning chances but from 5-3 at the interval I felt really good and won it 9-3, making 84 and 119 breaks in the last two frames.

---

1979 UK Championship
*Third Round* (Griffiths exempted until then)
Griffiths beat Cliff Wilson 9-4
89-40; 59-50; 36-93(91); 80(52)-30; 46(42)-66; 60(60)-42(42); 64(38)-47; 85-36; 0-83(79); 81(70)-1; 27-59; 77(34)-32; 72(39)-11

*Quarter-finals*
Griffiths beat Alex Higgins 9-7
25-90(57); 117(93)-26; 35-71(70); 85(40)-35; 71-29; 91(60)-9; 86(46)-36; 22-85(58); 20-54; 19-68; 5-83(76); 12-108(104); 60-20; 76(37)-39(38); 126(118)-0; 74(35)-16

*Semi-finals*
Griffiths beat Bill Werbeniuk 9-3
84(38)-46(40); 77(45)-52(44); 55(45)-70(58); 58(43)-64(35); 63(40)-17; 56-47(33); 17-81; 83(34)-30; 81-18; 77-32; 108(84)-30; 119(119)-4

---

During the day's gap before the final against John Virgo I went completely off the boil. I had no sense of thrill and anticipation inside me – which would certainly have been different if I had not been world champion – so it wasn't surprising that John was soon 5-0 up.

At his best, John is one of the very best players in the world. He has all the shots, plus a great deal of flair, and his only real weakness is his temperament. At times this can be very good, but at others he can get himself so screwed up inside that he can hardly pot a ball. Despite his ability he had won nothing big as an amateur and he had a habit of getting more and more worked up the closer he got to winning something important.

Underneath that beard of his, despite all his glowering and scowling, John can be very good company away from the table but there are times when he tries so hard that his game won't function. Against a player of his type you should dig in and make him sweat, but he was 7-1 up before I started to do that. My safety in particular had been very poor and I was letting John in so often that there was nothing to disturb his rhythm.

I niggled back to 5-7, but at 9-6 John won a crucial frame when he

John Virgo – Coral UK Champion 1979.

cleared up with 57 to win on the black to go 10-6. The last frame of the first day was also very important. I'd made a break of 71, my best of the day, to make it 7-10 and I was a few in front on the colours with a chance of making it 8-10. If I had won the frame to be only two behind with nine to play in the final session next day, it might have brought the best out of me – but John knocked in yellow to pink, so at 11-7 he was, in my mind, a strong favourite.

Throughout the tournament we had been starting the afternoon sessions at 1.45pm but in order to slot into BBC Television's *Grandstand* better we were due to start the last session at noon. John did not check the timetable so he was still resting at his hotel fifteen miles away when the phone rang.

He dived into his car, ran the last half mile to the Guildhall because of the traffic queues into the car park, and arrived thirty-one minutes late. The championship rules stated that he had to forfeit one frame for every fifteen minutes he was late. I think a fine would be more appropriate, and I asked for the two frames penalty to be waived – but rules were rules, apparently.

John was in a terrible state. He had worked all his life for a major title and now he could see it being snatched away from him. What made it worse was that he realised it was his own fault. He had been concentrating so hard on the match that nothing else had entered his head.

When we did start, he couldn't pot a ball. The penalty frames had made it 11-9 and two real frames made it 11-11 at the mid-session interval. I felt very badly about it all. Part of me wanted to win, but I knew I wouldn't be able to recognise it as such if I had not physically won all the frames which were credited to me on the scoreboard. I went into John's dressing-room and offered to share the prize money which was £4,500 for the winner and £2,250 for the runner-up. He said that he appreciated the offer but that he would rather play it out. There was no aggro at all between us.

The interval gave John a chance to pull himself together and he got one up again, but then I started to cue better than at any time in the match so far and knocked in two good clearances, 56 and 68, to go one up with two to play.

Still I didn't feel right. Part of me didn't want to win but it wasn't in me to give the match away. Because I was now cueing well, I knew that if I was left a chance for a break with balls open I wouldn't miss – but I hadn't got the determination to work for openings. When John won the last two frames I was quite relieved. I hadn't given them to him; he had earned them. I felt it was the right result.

John, full of confidence, went on to win another big tournament in Bombay immediately afterwards, beating Cliff Thorburn in the final, but by the time the world championship had come round in April this mood had gone and he lost to Eddie Charlton in the first round after

1979 UK Championship
*Final*
John Virgo beat Griffiths 14-13
I   70(38)-60(40);   67-9;   81(43,37)-24;   100(63,36)-24;
103(67)-26; 52-61; 73(69)-24; 96(30)-29; 22-90(44,31) (Virgo
7-2)
II   32-68;   4-126(60,48);   49-51;   86(39)-38(38);   50-59;
136(93)-3; 57(57)-56; 8-108(71); 55-45 (Virgo 11-7)
III   43-61;   50(30)-73;   65-44(31);   17-91(56);   26-96(68);
74(50)-19; 78-8; two frames forfeited to Griffiths by Virgo

missing countless chances. This could well be the story of John's life: he
is good enough to beat anybody but sometimes he can't beat himself.

A couple of weeks later (shortly after I had been elected 'Newcomer
of the Year' by the Sports Writers Association, the first time a snooker
player had won this kind of award) came the BBC's *Sports Review of the
Year* awards night. I had been invited to do a few trick shots while I was
chatting with Frank Bough. I was much more nervous than I would
have been if I had just been playing a match. To make it worse a couple
of things happened to cause me to have visions of my act being a
complete fiasco.

A match table usually takes a couple of hours to build, but the
demands of the programme were such that a ready-built table was
wheeled on. The secret of many trick shots lies entirely in how you set
the balls up. Do this properly and you can't miss. The Snake shot (see
drawing i) is one of these, but as I had less than a minute to set the balls
up I didn't set them up quite right.

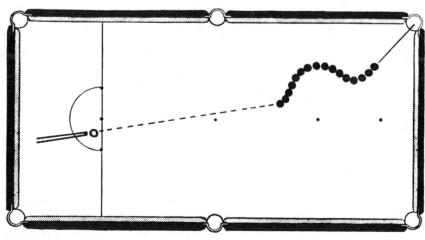

The Snake

'Of course', said Frank Bough, 'these work first time, every time, don't they?'

This one didn't.

The next one, the Grand National, so called because the balls jump over the butts of cues into the pocket (see drawing ii), I managed all right, but when I came to try my third trick (see drawing iii) I realised that the table was at least three inches too high.

You have to get the cue very high and strike downwards to get the cue-ball to jump over the 15 reds and through the triangle, but with those three extra inches to contend with I just got as high on my toes as I could and, balancing very unsteadily, hit the white quickly before I fell over. It had just about enough lift-off but I had also swerved it unintentionally. I could see it curving off-line but luckily it just caught the edge of the black and knocked it in.

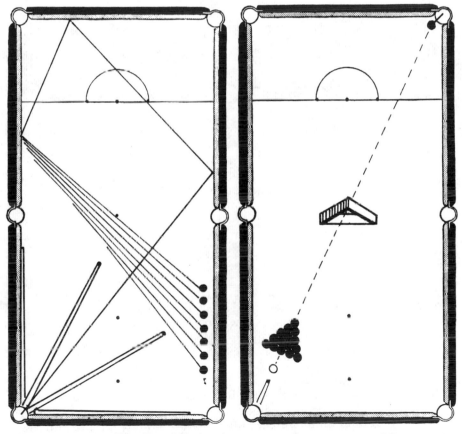

The Grand National                    The Triangle

Amazingly enough, all this went down very well. In those circumstances, I hadn't dared try any shots which required a high degree of skill, though I had worked hard on my trick shots just after I had turned professional. I worked about ten hours on the Machine Gun shot alone (see drawing iv). It took me about three hours to get it at all, and a lot longer before I could get it consistently.

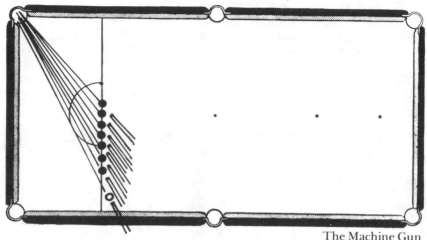

The Machine Gun

Christmas to the snooker professional means not only turkey and Christmas pudding but *Pot Black,* which is recorded in Birmingham over four days starting the day after Boxing Day. One of the reasons the standard of play is so low is that the players have let themselves go over Christmas, not just by eating and drinking, but mentally. It is very difficult to drop back into the right frame of mind immediately, particularly as the matches are only one frame each.

*Pot Black* was snooker's breakthrough with television and over the years it has been a shop window for the game. Until I played in it myself I did not realise how difficult it was for players to do themselves justice. The BBC in Birmingham just after Christmas is like a morgue. There is endless hanging about, the studio in which the matches are played does not have the right atmosphere, and much time is wasted on production details like rehearsing the introductions. In short, you hang about all day and are then expected to produce your best in only one frame.

Snooker is best on television when you have a proper tournament in a proper venue. The players play enough frames to get going and to allow the tension to build up. There is no real tension in *Pot Black* because all the players realise that it is a bit of a lottery. Everyone tries their best because the programme has a lot of viewers, and it is always better to be seen winning than losing – but in no way can the tournament be regarded as a true test of skill. A good run in *Pot Black* often means that players will be more in demand for club exhibitions, so much so that when Graham Miles won it as a late replacement in the early seventies it changed his life. If you already have as many bookings as you want, though, you can get the feeling that you are on a hiding to nothing. I didn't exactly get a hiding but I didn't reach the semi-finals.

Straight after this there was the Wilson's Classic in Manchester for Granada television, which did take place in a public venue but where the matches were again very short. I lost 2-0 to Higgins in the semi-finals and set off for London for, as I thought, a few club exhibitions and a meeting with my agent, Barrie Gill.

Driving me away from his office, he turned into a *cul-de-sac*. A bus pulled alongside and, as if I was dreaming, I saw it was full of people I knew. When the conductor turned out to be Eamonn Andrews I realised I was on *This Is Your Life*.

Eamonn Andrews springs the Big Red Book on me!

My next major commitment was the Woodpecker Welsh Professional Championship at Ebbw Vale Leisure Centre. I was drawn to play Doug Mountjoy in one semi-final with Ray Reardon to play Cliff Wilson in the other. The press had got a Griffiths v Reardon final all worked out, which would have been the first time we had met in competition, but Doug beat the pair of us for the title and the £2,250 first prize.

# CHAMPIONSHIP SNOOKER

It was my first real tournament since the end of November. I had been on the road almost constantly and I had had a lot on my plate with moving house, so I was really looking forward to it. Things had not been going too well for Doug. He had had a couple of disappointing results, he wasn't automatically getting invited into all the big tournaments, and a few gaps had started to appear in his diary which were not being filled by exhibition bookings. This may have been a blessing in disguise for him because when you are on the road there is little opportunity or time to practice.

Before the Welsh Professional Doug had been practising very hard but his confidence was still low when it came to our match. He snookered himself on the last red to let me in for a 30 clearance to win the first frame on the black, and he almost lost the second too after I had needed four snookers.

At this point, the referee said there would be an interval. It is ridiculous to have an interval after only two frames, but there was some problem with television timings which made it preferable to have the interval then rather than after three or four frames. If it had just been an ordinary tournament I would probably have accepted this, but if a national championship is at stake television's wishes have less weight. It was, to be fair, only a request and after a brief discussion we played on but for me the damage was done. Once my concentration had been affected, I should have taken the interval and used it to cool down but I just let it go.

Doug kept his concentration much better than I did and was 5-1 up before a 57 clearance and a 102 break pulled me up to 3-5 at the interval.

At 3-6, I made a 127 break and got up to 5-6. Needing a snooker with only pink and black left in the next, I laid a good one which Doug hit and went in-off. I had to pot pink in the middle at a very narrow angle and run through for the black. It was not an easy pot (diagram 46) and in making sure of it I finished short on the black. It was a thin cut and I left it in the jaws. Instead of 6-6 it was 7-5 to Doug.

Doug had been very shaky as I was catching up, but getting two up again gave him the boost he needed. He won 9-6 and beat Ray 9-6 in the final.

My first match in the Benson and Hedges Masters at Wembley Conference Centre was against Cliff Thorburn, who had beaten John Virgo 5-3 in the preliminary round from which I was exempt. Cliff, who is very well-liked in the snooker world, had been quoted, how accurately I don't know, as saying that he thought he was too soft, that he needed a harder personality and that, in effect, I had better watch out. This of course made me all the keener.

It was a very good match. Down 1-2, I potted an all-or-nothing pink and black (diagram 47) for 2-2. Cliff made a 96 in the next and was well

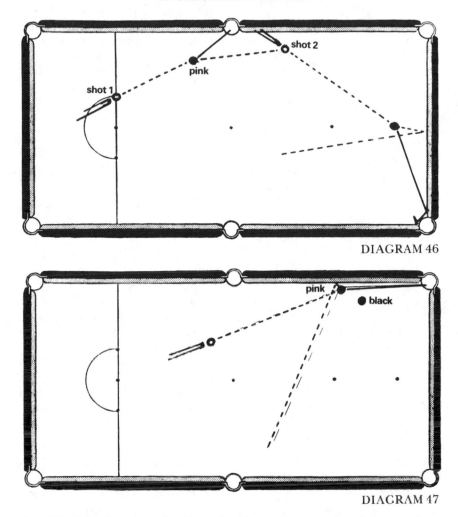

DIAGRAM 46

DIAGRAM 47

in with 41 in the next when he missed a very easy red and, next visit, a black off its spot. As I have said, he is inclined to make bad mistakes when he is trying to clinch matches or important leads. This frame would have put him two up with three to play, but I made a 73 clearance from his second mistake and made 64, 32 and 59 in the next two to win 5-3. I can't imagine anyone having an easy match against Cliff.

After I had nipped back to Cardiff to accept the Welsh Sports Personality of the Year award on BBC Wales, I played John Spencer in the semi-final. I've never seen John at his best because when he was at his peak in the early seventies my amateur career had hardly started. It is still obvious that he is a class player, but in the last few years he has been very inconsistent. I played pretty well, finishing up with 62, 77 and 100 in the last three frames, but John couldn't get going at all. I won 5-0 and Alex Higgins beat Ray Reardon 5-2 in the other semi-final.

---

**1980 Benson and Hedges Masters**
*Quarter-finals*
Griffiths beat Cliff Thorburn 5-3
73-61(37);  13-77(62);  29-78(30);  57(38)-54;  14-120(96); 97(73)-42(41); 80(64)-35; 121(32,59)-15

*Semi-finals*
Griffiths beat John Spencer 5-0
105(36,54)-11; 65-52; 84(62)-8; 83(77)-40; 104(100)-11

---

Like our quarter-finals in the world and UK championships, this was another good match. Maybe it is because we are complete opposites that we seem to bring out the best in each other. Alex drinks: I'm teetotal. Alex is a great one for cards, casinos and horses: I don't gamble at all. He likes to live it up: I like peace and quiet.

Alex has got a nice side but he can be very irritating. Everybody likes to shine, but the limelight means so much to him that he forgets everything else. I had long since refused to play any more exhibitions with him because he had made it very clear that he wanted to do all the entertaining. He had also made it clear in some matches that he wanted to do the refereeing as well. He is very fair-minded in declaring fouls on himself which the referee has not seen, but if a decision goes against him which he does not agree with he is inclined to give the referee a mouthful of abuse. He had already been fined £250, the maximum, for 'foul and abusive language to referees and bringing the game into disrepute' and by the end of the season there were three other incidents which cost him another £250. I can do without being involved in this sort of aggravation and so I decided that I would play him only when the draw brought us together in tournaments.

Strangely enough, I enjoy playing him in matches. He plays a very positive game and you have to be on your toes all the time. Something about him – his attitude or the way he plays – always gets the crowd going, so there's plenty of atmosphere too. The sort of supporters I have sit quietly at the back, say nothing and go home, while Alex's are shouting as if it is a football match. I love all this in a big venue and it usually brings the best out of me.

I led 2-0, but Alex got on the warpath in the third with a break of 81 (which was timed at four minutes) and won the fourth on a re-spot black. He played the perfect break-off, cue-ball on the side cushion, black on the baulk cushion (diagram 48). I got the double kiss attempting the safety shot and left the black easy for him.

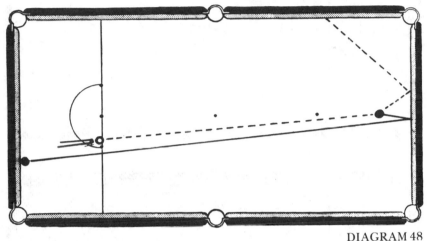

DIAGRAM 48

At 3-2 I missed a straightforward clear-up to lead 4-2. All I had to do was stroke the blue in from its spot and run the cue-ball off the top and side cushions to get on the pink, but somehow I missed it.

I threw the next frame away as well, missing a straight pink from its spot for game so instead of being 5-2 up I was 3-4 down. In the circumstances, I was very pleased to play the last frame of the afternoon as well as I did to make it 4-4 at the interval.

The first frame of the evening was crucial. Alex was 52 in front with three reds left, but in taking the yellow after the fourth last red he knocked the brown in and left me a free ball. I cleared up with 53 to win on the black.

Although I still had to pot the balls, this had to be reckoned as a frame Alex had thrown away – just as I had thrown two away in the afternoon.

At 7-5 Alex did almost the same thing when he was 39 in front with only one red left. He tried the red at speed, went in-off and I tied the game with a 35 clearance.

Alex played the opening shot at the black perfectly, just as he had in the afternoon, but I had learned from the experience of playing the identical shot earlier and this time managed the right reply (diagram 49 – see next page). Eventually I doubled the black round into the middle pocket off three cushions (diagram 50, next page) to lead 8-5.

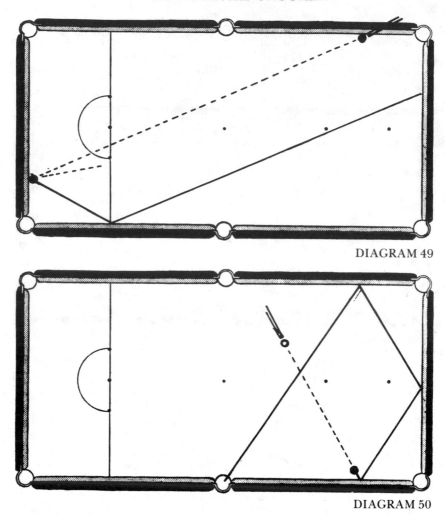

DIAGRAM 49

DIAGRAM 50

The next frame I had first chance, and knocked the lot in for 131. With the world championship only a couple of months away, I had desperately needed to win a tournament and I had done so. It was the best match I had played since the championship, and it gave me the feeling that I might retain it. By the time the championship actually came round, it was a different story.

The following week, I won the Benson and Hedges Irish Masters, beating Doug 10-9 in a mediocre final in which I led 8-4 and trailed 8-9. But the rot set in at the British Gold Cup, a new event at Derby Assembly Rooms.

The format was that each player played three frames against each of

---

**1980 Benson and Hedges Masters**
*Final*
Griffiths beat Alex Higgins 9-5
67-39; 73(73)-30; 4-81(81); 61(38)-68(33); 104(77)-15;
61(52)-67(33); 54(36)-55(35); 102(39)-25; 66(53)-61(39);
58(58)-70(70); 75-49; 117(51,42)-3; 67(35)-60(38); 131(131)-0

---

the other three players in his group. I beat Patsy Fagan 3-0 and David Taylor 2-1; Alex had lost 2-1 to David and beaten Patsy 2-1, so when it came to the last match he had to beat me 3-0 to win the group.

I missed a good chance to clinch the first frame and Alex won it on the black with a 42 clearance. This gave him just the encouragement he needed. A total clearance of 135 gave him the next and a 14-red clearance of 134 the last. It was a terrific performance and the first time, I understand, that consecutive breaks of over 130 had been made in tournament play. Alex went on to win the tournament, beating Ray Reardon 5-1 in the final.

After this, I slipped steadily downhill. I went from Derby to Ipswich for the Tolly Cobbold tournament which was covered by Anglia Television. I had no form at all. At the time I put it down to being jaded through too much dashing about. I was glad I had no more tournament commitments for a few weeks, and I had deliberately not accepted many exhibition bookings.

So I had a long build-up to the world championship: too long. I gave myself time to prepare, I practised, I was physically rested – but I didn't feel right. Perhaps I needed more than a few weeks to undo the stress and strain of nearly a year because nothing that I could do seemed to reduce the tension I was feeling. I was in exactly the opposite position to the one I had been in a year before. As champion I had everything to lose and nothing to gain; the only way I could go was down.

It also occurred to me that if I won again I would be in for another hectic year full of pressure and hassle and not seeing as much of Annette and the boys as I wanted. This would never influence me not to try my hardest and, of course, the desire to remain champion overrode everything else – but if there is the smallest corner of your subconscious which is not committed to winning it can make a difference.

I wasn't happy with my draw. As champion I was seeded through to the last sixteen at Sheffield to play either Steve Davis or Patsy Fagan. Two or three years previously, this might well have been Patsy, but after winning the first couple of frames he faded out and Steve won 10-6, not a close finish but enough to make Steve feel that he had played a real match and got attuned to the atmosphere of the Crucible. The two match tables were also different in many respects from those used in 1979: the cushions were very springy and the cloth was thinner with less nap, thus making it more difficult to 'hold' screwshots of half-ball or slightly less. Steve had adjusted to this before he played me, and because I was out of touch anyway it took me longer to adjust than it should have done.

On top of everything else, I knew what a good player Steve was. On his home table in the Romford Lucania match room he had given me – and just about everyone else – a real going over and, though he hadn't done quite so well in the big tournaments as his supporters had expected, he'd done well enough for me to realise that my first match could well be my hardest.

Steve's technique is as near perfect as anyone is likely to see. His cue action is very smooth and straight, he keeps completely still on his shot, he knows all the moves. Once he gets into his rhythm, it seems that all he has to do is switch on automatic pilot and just reel off the frames. The only solution is either to beat him to the punch or play well enough to put a touch of anxiety or uncertainty in his mind.

As it was, I played right into his hands. The build-up to defending the title had gone on so long that it was a relief to start playing. When I walked out I was perfectly relaxed. I was still relaxed when I was 7-0 down: I just wasn't potting any balls. Steve was in the position I had been in the previous year – an unknown, as far as the general public was concerned, tackling an established player with, he knew, a good chance of causing an upset. He was keyed up for the occasion, and cashed in on my mistakes, playing better and better. I managed to win the last frame of that first session but at 7-1 down overnight I was in real trouble.

Steve had not given me enough chances to get my game going, and I had hardly knocked in any of the 50-50 or 40-60 opening pots you need to get in at this level. On the second day, I had a bit more feeling but at 1-8 and 3-10 I was seven frames behind, one more than I had been overnight. My approach had improved, though, in that I was just playing snooker without letting my mind dwell on the score. On the other hand, I think it suddenly occurred to Steve that he was getting close to winning and he went just a shade tense, missing a few of the long pots that he had been getting consistently and making the occasional mistake when he was in.

I kept plugging away, and won the last three frames of the day to pull up to 6-10. Overall, I was disappointed to win this session only 5-3, but at four behind I still had a glimmer of a chance. Steve was still favourite of course, but he had all night to reflect that four in front wasn't as good as seven in front had been.

Next morning, I felt very good. I won the first frame and the second as well after Steve had been first in with 40. His break had ended at what was quite an easy pot but he had to take the cue-ball through a cluster of reds and his position was uncertain. Sometimes your posi-

tional calculations can become so complicated that you don't devote enough attention to the pot. It is as if the mind is overloaded. When Steve missed, I made 67 and played safe on the last red. Steve messed up the safety shot and I made it 10-8.

Steve was cracking a bit, as most players do when a big lead has almost dwindled away. His cue action is so good that he was still potting balls, but his touch had deteriorated so that he wasn't stringing breaks together or putting the cue-ball in quite the place he wanted with his safety shots. I made it 10-9 and in the next frame I made a 90 break off a fluke!

The mid-session interval came at a bad time for me. I had won all four frames that morning – plus the last three of the night before – so I had a charge going. It would have been in my interests to keep playing. Steve, on the other hand, badly needed a few minutes to compose himself.

He said afterwards that when I made it 10-10 he felt that some of the pressure was off him. Nevertheless, if I had won the first frame after the interval, I think it is very unlikely that I would have lost. Steve led 16-0 but then I got in with the balls well set for a winning break.

With four reds left, I had made 51 (see diagram 51, shot 1). I took the black – 58 – intending to take the cue-ball off the top cushion and on to the red which was directly between the pink and black spots. Unless I was much too slow and finished almost touching the red, which was very unlikely on the fast cloth we were playing on, I was certain to be on at least one red into a middle pocket with the other three in open positions for a clearance.

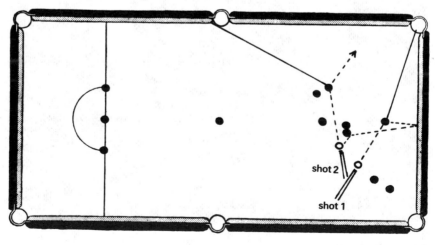

DIAGRAM 51

I used a shade too much right-hand side so the cue-ball, as shown, brushed the red next to the one I was aiming for. I couldn't pot either of the reds between the pink and black; I couldn't pot the red next to the pink because the pink was in the way; so I had to attempt the other red at a more acute angle into the middle pocket (diagram 51, shot 2). I have always hated these slow drops into the middle pocket. Perhaps because I was brought up on tables with thick naps which allow a slow, middle-pocket pot against the nap to curl into the pocket, my instinct and preference is to aim for the far jaw and let the nap do the rest. The cloth used for the championship this year, though, had a very short nap so this sort of pot went straight. I aimed for the far jaw and hit the far jaw.

I didn't lose the frame solely through this, but it meant that I had missed my chance. Steve also fell down when he made 17 and missed an easy blue (diagram 52). He didn't need to hit it hard, but instead of playing the pot positively he almost rolled it and left it in the jaws.

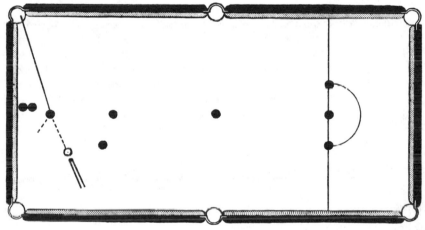

DIAGRAM 52

If I had been thinking clearly, I would have realised the supreme importance, with Steve rocking, of making him work for his chances. I should have been ready to close up the game at the first sign of danger but I didn't even think of it. I thought there was just enough room between the blue and the jaw of the pocket to squeeze the last red in (diagram 53, next page). It turned out that there wasn't, and with the red over the pocket for starters Steve cleared up to lead 11-10.

This was just what he needed to restore his confidence. The next frame, he made a 116 break so I was two down with three to play. Countless matches have been won from this position – but instead of thinking how difficult it was going to be for him to win the frame he

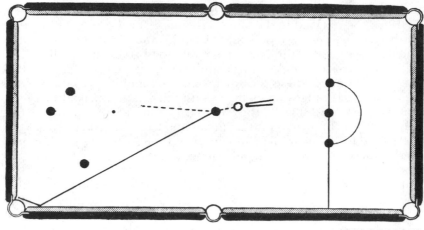

DIAGRAM 53

needed, all I could think of was how difficult it was going to be for me to win three. I was still well in the match but thinking as if I was out of it.

I was down 59-0 when I got in with 22, missing a red along the top cushion (diagram 54) because I was still kicking myself for leaving it an awkward half-ball when it had been an easy stun from the black to leave it threequarter-ball, which would have been much easier. I didn't expect to have another shot. But Steve ran out of position in potting the red I had left and had to settle for taking the pink with no position to leave himself 44 in front with only two reds left. I needed a snooker.

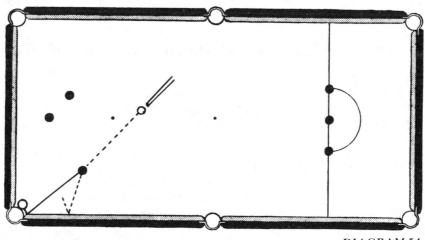

DIAGRAM 54

I got the last two reds, but when he took the yellow to go 32 in front I was sure it was the end. Somehow, he missed an easy green. I got one of the snookers I needed and then, when I gave him another, he went in-off the brown. Suddenly I could win but somehow I hadn't got it in me. I took the brown in the middle pocket but missed my position (diagram 55) on the blue by nearly a yard! I struggled on, playing automatically, but misjudged a safety shot on the blue. At this stage, I couldn't win the match but Steve could still lose it.

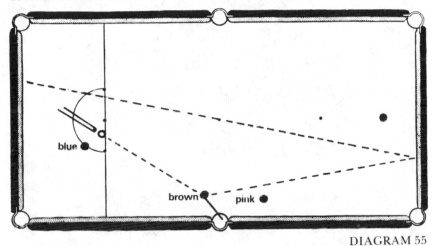

DIAGRAM 55

He almost went in-off potting the blue, but this meant that I needed snookers again, and all he had to do was roll the pink down the side cushion not caring whether it went in, which it did, or not.

'What are his strengths?' David Vine asked me about Steve in the after-match interview.

'His strengths? I've spent the last three days trying to find a weakness.'

It was true. Steve had played well but when it came to the crunch I

1980 World Championship
*Second Round* (Griffiths exempted from first)
Steve Davis beat Griffiths 13-10
I   85-26;   62-54(35);   79(75)-15;   77(58)-25;   72(44)-33;
103(30,50)-1; 94(61)-0; 32-73(60) (Davis 7-1)
II   69(36)-37;  35-73;  16-80(40);  70(35)-17;  113(59,50) 17,
40-58(38); 49(41)-90(32,52); 5-81(44) (Davis 10-6)
III   42-74(43);   40(40)-98(67,31);   57(40)-73;   11-96(90);
67(34)-58(58); 116(116)-5; 78-51

The reign ends ...

felt that I could still have won if I could have held my game together.
This is snooker though. Nobody can play to their peak form all the time
and at least I had picked myself up enough to make Steve win the
match rather than hand it to him on a plate as I had looked like doing at
the start. Over the three sessions, I had simply not played well enough.

Steve in turn faded at the wrong time against Alex in the quarter-
finals and lost 13-9. Alex threw his chance away in the final when he led
by four frames on the first day, only for Cliff to level overnight. Cliff, it
seemed, had thrown his chance away when he missed a very easy brown
which would have put him two up with three to play, but showed his
character by putting this behind him to win the next two frames for the
title.

# A CHAMPION'S YEAR

At top level, a few good shots or a couple of mistakes can make so much difference. That is what makes snooker so exciting to watch, and why the pressure, even if you are not always conscious of it, is so great.

I was disappointed, though not as much as I was when it sank in more fully a few days later that I was no longer champion – and not as much as I would have been if I had not won the championship the previous year.

'It's not the end of the world', I said in one interview. 'It's just the end of the world championship for me for this year.'

. . . but the journey never ends.